Your Puppy, Your Dog

A Kid's Guide to Raising a Happy, Healthy Dog

Pat Storer

STOREY
BOOKS
Schoolhouse Road
Pownal, Vermont 05261

D1122346

The mission of Storey Communications is to serve our customers
by publishing practical information that encourages personal independence
in harmony with the environment.

Edited by Lorin Driggs
Cover design by Carol J. Jessop and Susan Bernier
Cover photograph by A. Blake Gardner
Text design and production by Susan Bernier
Photographs by Pat Storer, Isabelle Francais/Pet Profiles, Kent and Donna Dannen,
   and Pets by Paulette
Line drawings by Jeffrey C. Domm, except for pages 26–28, by Brigita Fuhrmann
Technical review by James M. Leahey, D.V.M.
Indexed by Susan Olason

Copyright © 1997 Patricia J. Storer

The information in this book is true and complete to the best of our knowledge. All
recommendations are made without guarantee on the part of the author or Storey Books.
The author and publisher disclaim any liability in connection with the use of this information. For additional information, please contact Storey Books, Schoolhouse Road, Pownal,
Vermont 05261.

Storey Books are available for special premium and promotional uses and for customized
editions. For further information, please call Storey's Custom Publishing Department
at 1-800-793-9396.

Printed in the United States by Capital City Press
10 9 8 7 6 5 4

Library of Congress Cataloging-in-Publication Data

Storer, Pat
      Your puppy, your dog : a kid's guide to raising a happy, healthy dog / by
      Pat Storer.
            p.   cm.

      ISBN 0-88266-959-1 (pbk. : alk. paper)
      1. Dogs—Juvenile literature. [1. Dogs. 2. Pets] I. Title.
SF426.5.S77 1997
636.7'0087—dc20   97-5725
                                                                                    CIP

contents

Introduction

We can only guess how a human and a dog first developed a lasting relationship over 10,000 years ago. No one knows for sure, but it's very likely that some orphaned wolf pups were taken in and raised by a prehistoric human tribe. A bond formed, and the two species became loyal companions. From that distant time until today, something wonderful happens when that bond of mutual trust and love develops.

To the Parent:

Kids and puppies go together like bread and butter. Both have lots of love to share, and they will teach each other many things. Caring for a dog can be a remarkable learning and loving experience.

The decision to add a puppy or a dog to your child's life should be made by the whole family. Both the child and the family must be willing to accept a 10- to 15-year commitment to the care and well-being of the dog.

First and foremost, the dog should be welcomed as another member of the family. Like people, dogs are social creatures and cannot thrive in isolation. To be his best, a dog needs to be treated with kindness and respect. You should be available to guide your child when needed and to oversee your child's treatment and training of the puppy or dog.

Caring and Learning

Caring for a puppy or dog is a wonderful opportunity for a child to learn to be responsible. However, the dog's health and well-being should never be compromised in order to teach a lesson in responsibility.

To the Child:

You probably already know deep in your heart that you really want a dog of your own. But there are some things you should think about before you make the final decision.

With the pleasure a dog can bring come duties and responsibilities. If you are 10 years old, the puppy you get now will grow up into a dog that may be around after you have graduated from both high school and college. For all of those years your dog will rely upon you for food, shelter, health care, and companionship.

Because a dog is a natural follower, he will look to you for direction. It will be up to you to train him and teach him what he needs to know. You must be patient and understanding while your puppy or dog is learning what you want of him. You must be kind and fair if he does something wrong. Usually, a puppy makes a mistake because he doesn't understand what he's supposed to do.

A dog is an intelligent creature with real feelings and definite emotional needs. He can feel happy or sad, afraid or brave, confident or confused. The way you treat and train your dog will have a large impact on how he will develop physically and emotionally. The puppy can grow up to be a happy and a pleasant member of your family and community. He can also grow up to be a spoiled brat — even neurotic — displaying habits that no one enjoys. The outcome is up to you. You must choose the type of dog that is best suited to your lifestyle. You must teach him, care for him, love him, and play with him. I am going to show you how to do that.

About "He" and "She"

In this book, "he" or "him" is used to refer to a dog, unless something specific to female dogs is being discussed. However, the information in the book is true for both male and female dogs.

A dog is a great friend.

Choosing the Best Dog for You

Here are some things to think about before you make the final decision to get a dog:

- A cute little puppy will grow up into a dog that can live 15 years or more.

- A dog costs money — the purchase price, food, *neutering,* housing, health care, toys, training equipment, boarding, and even training.

- You must provide your dog with fresh water and nutritious food every day.

- You must provide a safe, comfortable place for your dog to live.

- You must walk an apartment dog at least twice a day.

- You must be sure a house dog has access to a protected area outside, or you must walk him at least twice a day.

- Your must give your dog exercise, play, and lots of love and affection.

- You must be willing to discipline your dog firmly and fairly when necessary.

Neutering. A surgical procedure that makes an animal unable to breed.

- You must clean up after your dog, no matter where he relieves himself.

- You must check your dog every day to be certain he's healthy.

- You must brush, comb, and bathe your dog, and trim his nails regularly.

- You must teach him everything he needs to know to be a good citizen.

- You must socialize him with your friends and other dogs.

- You will be responsible if your dog causes problems for anyone or damages anything.

- You must have a good health program for your dog, including vaccinations, flea control, and de-worming.

- You must abide by all laws and rules of your state, county, city, subdivision, or apartment concerning dog ownership.

- You must be willing to neuter your dog.

Love and good care will help a dog live to a ripe old age.

Your Lifestyle and Your Dog

If you are still sure that you really want to add a dog to your life, there are certain things you need to think about before you choose your dog. The answers to the following questions will help you find the dog that's right for you.

1. How active are *you* and what do you enjoy doing in your free time? Do you like to run, swim, bike, hike, or play ball? Do you spend your spare time reading, watching TV, playing chess or video games, surfing the Internet?

2. Do you live in the country, a suburb, or a city? Do you live in a house or apartment? Will the dog live inside your home or have a place of his own outside?

3. What ages are the other members of your family? Are there any babies or very young children? Are there any physically challenged people in the family? Are they all okay with the idea of your having a dog?

4. Do you have other family pets?

5. Do other dogs live nearby? Do the neighbors keep their dogs under control?

6. Do you want to participate in events with your dog, such as obedience, carting, or tracking?

7. Do you have the extra time to groom a long-haired dog, or would a short-coated breed be a better choice?

8. How much money do you plan to spend on the purchase of your dog?

What Do Those Dog Terms Mean?

There are many similar terms that refer to a dog's status in the world of dogs. People are often confused about these words and may accidentally use the wrong one.

Purebred

A *purebred* dog is one whose parents are both of the same recognized breed — for example, both parents are Collies or both parents are Dalmatians. Some people also use the term *thoroughbred* (which usually refers to horses) or *blue-blood* (especially in hounds).

A purebred dog can make a wonderful companion.

Registered

A *registered* dog is one that's purebred and has a record of his birth and his parents' births kept by an organization specializing in registering dogs. For example, both parents are registered German Shepherds and the litter has been registered with the appropriate *kennel club* or *breed club,* the puppies are considered registered.

Pedigreed

A *pedigree* is a record of a dog's ancestors, usually written as a family tree. Some breeders furnish a pedigree of their own. A certified pedigree can also be ordered from the kennel or breed club with which the dog is registered. A *pedigreed* dog is one for which such an ancestry record has been kept. He may or may not be registered.

Kennel *or* **breed club.** *An organization that maintains pedigrees and other records of dogs that are registered with the club.*

Mongrel *or* **mutt.** *A mixed-breed dog.*

Mixed Breed

A *mixed-breed* dog is one whose parents are from more than one recognized breed or from undetermined parentage. For example, his father might be a Labrador Retriever and his mother an Irish Setter, or one or both of his parents themselves might be mixed breeds. Many times no one has any idea what a dog's ancestors were, because as far back as anyone can remember, they were mixed breeds. Mixed-breed dogs are sometimes called *mongrels* or *mutts.*

Crossbred

A *crossbred* dog is one whose parents are of two (or more) different breeds, but their mating was planned deliberately by professional breeders to produce a new breed.

A mixed breed can give as much love as a purebred.

Inbred or Linebred

Inbred or *linebred* dogs are those whose parents are of the same breed and closely related by family kinship. Experienced dog breeders mate such dogs to reinforce particular inherited traits.

Mixed Breed or Pure Breed?

Now that you understand what all of those dog terms mean, you're ready to make an important decision. Will your new dog be a mixed breed or a pure breed?

Mixed Breeds

A mixed-breed puppy or dog's parents are not of the same breed. You may not be able to find out what breed or mixture of breeds his parents are. If he's a puppy, you may have to guess what he will look like as an adult, how large he will get, and what characteristics he may have inherited from his parents. A cute, cuddly little puppy of eight weeks might turn out to weigh 10 pounds — or 100 pounds. He might have an inherited instinct and desire to herd your neighbor's sheep or chase cars when you aren't paying attention.

Mixed breeds generally seem to have fewer of the inherited health problems that are common in certain pure breeds. These problems include deafness, early cancer, and *hip dysplasia.* Mixed breeds probably have fewer inherited health problems because both parents are not the same breed and are less apt to carry the matching problem *genes.*

Today, there are organizations that allow mixed breeds to compete in nearly all activities available to purebred dogs, with the exception of conformation.

How Big Will that Mixed-Breed Puppy Get?

One way to get an idea of whether a puppy will grow up into a large or small dog is to look at his bone structure, especially in his legs and paws. A puppy with a large bone structure and heavy legs and paws will most likely grow up to be much larger and heavier than one of the same age with fine bones and small legs and paws. Some breeds that have a fine bone structure, however, grow up to be very tall; the Greyhound is an example.

Some mongrels show the characteristics of several breeds.

Pure Breeds

Purebred dogs were bred by people to have specific characteristics of structure, hair coat, color, size, abilities, and temperament.

The genetic makeup of the dog is easily changed by selective breeding. By choosing particular physical and character traits, and then breeding dogs that have those traits, people have developed purebred dogs that can perform amazing feats.

Dogs have been specially bred to hunt *game,* track prisoners, pull wagons, guard and defend property and people, herd cattle and sheep, work with police, run races, retrieve or point to game birds, protect livestock, sniff for drugs and other illegal items, dig out badgers, seek out rats, provide companionship, and more.

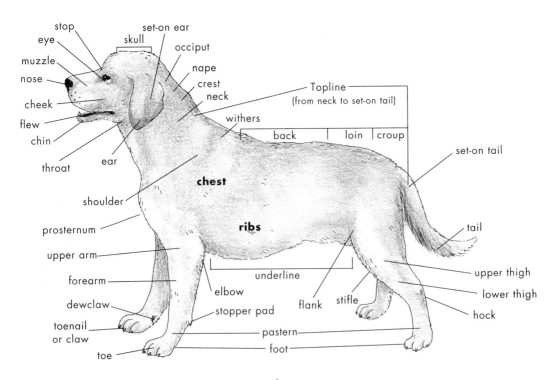

Parts of a Dog

With a purebred puppy, you know what he will look like when he grows up, and about how big he will get. If you choose a breed that was developed for a specific trait, remember that your dog will have this trait bred into him also. You might even decide to develop this inherited trait to have more fun with your dog. There's a national club for nearly every breed of dog, unless it's very rare. Most of these clubs are ready and happy to give you information on the potential of that particular breed. (See "Helpful Sources," pages 161–162.)

Breed Groups

Dog breeds are organized into categories or groups based on the breeds' main traits. If you're getting a purebred dog, knowing the characteristics of the different groups can help you narrow your choices. The American Kennel Club (AKC) is the most widely recognized kennel club in the United States. There are seven groups of dogs in the AKC system. (See pages 159–160 for a complete listing of breeds by groups.)

Sporting

The dogs in this group were developed to show where game is by pointing, to flush game out from where it's hiding, or to retrieve game that has been killed. They include all pointers, setters, retrievers, and most spaniels. They are active dogs for active people. They make good companions if you like to hike or bike or have the time to help them spend their boundless energy. These dogs are happiest when they are active.

Many Breeds

Well over 500 breeds of dogs have been developed over the years. Some are now extinct or have been developed into different breeds.

Sporting group:
Chesapeake Bay Retriever

Sporting group:
Weimaraner

Non-sporting group:
Chinese Shar-Pei

Non-sporting group:
Boston Terrier

Non-Sporting

This group includes such breeds as the Bichon Frise, Boston Terrier, Bulldog, Chow Chow, Dalmatian, Schipperke, and Miniature and Standard Poodles. Most of the breeds in this group were originally developed for specific working traits, but became so favored as companion dogs and pets that they are no longer used for their original jobs. The Dalmatian was originally used as a coach dog; it's now a popular mascot of many fire stations. Bulldogs were once fierce dogs that were used to tease bulls and make them charge. Although they are affectionate companions, bulldogs still have the instincts for which they were bred and may not be good around other animals.

Working

This group of dogs was bred to work for a living. They can work closely with people and include breeds used for pulling sleds and carts; search and rescue; and guarding people, property, and livestock. Among the Working group are Boxers, Dobermans, Great Danes, Rottweilers, Saint Bernards, Siberian Huskies, and the two larger sizes of Schnauzers. Many of these dogs are large. Properly chosen and trained, they make great family dogs and can become protective of their owners. Some of the

Working group:
Alaskan Malamute

Working group: Great Pyrenees

breeds can be aggressive to other dogs and people outside the family, however. It's very important to choose wisely in this and other groups; pick puppies whose parents have even and stable temperaments.

Herding

This group was bred to herd cattle or sheep (and sometimes poultry). It includes the Australian Cattle Dog, Australian Shepherd, Collie, Briard, Puli, German Shepherd, Shetland Sheepdog, Welsh Corgi, and others. The herding instinct is still strong in many individuals in this group; they will try to gather chickens, ducks, and even people into a group.

Hound

The dogs in this group were bred as *sight* or *scent hounds.* That means they track and follow their game by using their eyes or their noses. They range in size from the Dachshund to the Irish Wolfhound. The two basic types of hounds differ in temperament and physical characteristics. The sight hounds, bred to follow their prey by sight, are streamlined, with long, narrow muzzles. Some sight hounds tend to be aloof to unfamiliar people and are often content with very

Herding group:
Collie (rough coat)

Herding group:
German Shepherd

Hound group: Beagle

Hound group: Whippet

Terrier group: American Staffordshire Terrier

Terrier group: West Highland Terrier

Toy group: Miniature Pinscher

little attention. Even though many of them are quite large, they do quite well in an apartment or home. Scent hounds live in a world of smells and odors, most of them too irresistible not to be checked out. They often seem oblivious to the rest of the world when they come upon a trail or smell that intrigues them. They have deep baying voices that they use to express their feelings and communicate with each other. This group includes the Beagle, the Basset Hound, and the Bloodhound.

Terrier

This group includes all terriers except those few that are included in the Toy and Non-Sporting groups. Among them are the Airedale, Bedlington, Fox, Kerry Blue, Scottish, and Welsh. Terriers are bundles of limitless energy ready at all times to jump, bounce, and cavort. They are not quiet dogs and need to be trained at an early age to curb this trait. They were bred to be brave and to chase rats and other pests into their ground nests, where they held or killed them. This instinct is still strong in them today. They are also aggressive to other dogs and extremely protective of their property.

Toy

This group includes the small companion-type dogs such as the Chihuahua, Japanese Chin, Maltese, Papillon, Pug, Toy Poodle, and Yorkshire Terrier. There's even a hairless breed, the Chinese Crested, in this group. Toys are the tiniest of the purebred dogs and very suitable for small living quarters. Some of these breeds are more delicate than dogs in other groups and might not be a good choice for a family with rambunctious children. Some toy dogs are noisy and need to be shown at a young age that this behavior is not desirable in your home. This trait can be a positive one, however, because their alert attitude helps them to be good watchdogs.

Toy group: Pomeranian

Male or Female?

Another decision you may need to make is whether your new dog will be a male or a female. If you plan to neuter (also called *castration*) a male or *spay* a female, it really won't make much difference whether you pick a male or a female puppy. (See chapter 5, page 89, to find out about spaying and neutering.) If the animal you're going to adopt is an adult, he or she may have already developed habits peculiar to that sex. Males may hike their legs and urinate anywhere and every-where. Females may be overly submissive and urinate when they are excited. Neutering or spaying a dog that has already developed these habits might not change the established behavior.

Castration. Removing the testicles of a male dog so that he can't breed.

Spay. To remove the ovaries and uterus of a female dog so that she can't breed.

About Males

A male that isn't neutered will be more apt to "mark" his territory, including inside the house, with urine. He will want to mate with any female that's in *heat* within the range of his sense of smell. Unneutered male dogs tend to be roamers. Many don't tolerate other male dogs very well. Males that have not been neutered can develop serious diseases and injuries to the reproductive tract.

Heat. The time in a female dog's reproductive cycle when she is ready to mate and become pregnant.

You Can Save a Life!

There are many good reasons for adopting from an animal shelter. The shelters try very hard to find homes for all of the animals they receive. But, sadly, they receive many more animals than they can find people to adopt them. Some shelters have a maximum length of time that they can house an animal. If an animal isn't adopted by the time that period is up, he is euthanized, or "put to sleep." If you choose a dog or puppy from a shelter, you have actually just saved a life!

Euthanize. To humanely end the life of an animal, usually by giving it an injection.

About Females

A female that isn't spayed will usually come into heat every four to six months. During this time there's a bloody discharge from her *vulva*. She will attract male dogs that will try to mate with her. During the beginning and end of her cycle, she may be irritable and not want anyone around her rear. In the few days during the cycle when she's actually ready for breeding, she will want to mate. If she gets out and finds a male, she *will* mate.

An unspayed female that isn't bred may have a false pregnancy. She will exhibit all of the symptoms of a real pregnancy — sometimes even a "pretend" *labor*. Real pregnancies last about two months, but a false pregnancy can last up to three months. Unspayed females can also develop uterine infections, mammary tumors, and other diseases of the reproductive tract.

Where to Get a Puppy or Dog

Where you get your puppy or dog depends to some extent on whether you want a mixed breed or a pure breed. Puppies and dogs can be obtained from animal shelters, breed rescue organizations, individual breeders, kennels, and pet stores.

Animal Shelters

Animal shelters include the Humane Society, Society for the Prevention of Cruelty to Animals, city and county pounds, and various other animal protection agencies. Puppies and dogs found at shelters are often mixed breeds that have been donated to that organization because the owners could no longer care for them. Some are strays whose owners cannot be located.

Most shelters have a routine health check for the animals they offer for adoption. This may include immunizations, parasite checks, and treatment.

Shelters require that all animals placed for adoption be spayed or neutered. If the animal is too young for the surgery at the time of adoption, shelters require that you have it done by a stated date. Most medium-size and larger cities have clinics that specialize in low-cost neutering.

The price for an adoption from an animal shelter is very low considering all of the work that shelters do. They often have helpful literature for pet owners and may even have free educational programs that you and your parents may attend. Some shelters offer a program that lets kids in the community volunteer to help socialize puppies and kittens. This might be a good chance for you to "try out" a puppy or dog before you take him home. At the same time, you'll be performing a valuable community service. (See pages 155–157 for more information on volunteering.)

You will see a variety of purebred and mixed-breed puppies and dogs at an animal shelter.

A large majority of the dogs and puppies at shelters are mixed breeds. You will find some purebred adult dogs, but it's uncommon for shelters to have purebred puppies for adoption.

An adult dog might seem to be the perfect pet because you know what he looks like as an adult, what size he is, and his personality. You may find an adult dog that has been trained to be obedient, is already house trained, and might even know some tricks. However, an adult dog may have been turned over to a shelter because he has problems that the owners didn't like, such as nuisance barking, digging, or chasing cars. The dog might have been mistreated, allowed to run wild, or spoiled to the point that he isn't an enjoyable pet. He might not have had proper health care or nutrition while he was growing up; this may show up as health problems later on. An adult dog might have behaviors that you aren't experienced enough to deal with or that require training to correct.

Some shelters allow you to bring back a "problem dog" within a certain time period and exchange him for another animal. If you decide on an older dog, ask what your options are if the dog doesn't work out because of established behavior problems that aren't suitable for you and your family.

If you decide to adopt from a shelter, a young puppy might be the best choice. You both will be starting out fresh, and the pup won't have already formed bad habits. If the puppy is a mixed breed, it may be difficult to predict what he will look like as an adult. Size is another thing that can surprise you.

Breed Rescue Organizations

Single-breed rescue organizations specialize in one breed of dog. Not all of them operate in the same way, because they are individually run and funded. Most of them take in dogs of their specified breed, have them health checked and neutered or spayed, then adopt

Take Your Time

Be sure to check out all of the shelters in your area before you make a decision. Don't feel that you have to take a puppy the first time you visit. Shelters get new puppies frequently, so you'll be able to pick the right dog if you're patient and take your time.

them out to good homes. If you're interested in a dog of a particular breed, check with the national club for that breed. (The American Kennel Club has a listing of the national clubs for the breeds it recognizes.) The national club will have a list of rescue organizations for its breed in your area.

Pet Stores

Pet stores buy their puppies from commercial kennels instead of from local breeders. This makes it impossible for you to view the parents. Reputable pet stores give buyers a contract. If you buy a puppy from a pet store, make sure that you get a contract and that you read it carefully to see how you're protected if the puppy has problems. Some commercial kennels have good breeding practices and produce puppies that make wonderful pets. Others may not be as reliable and may produce puppies with hereditary defects. You need to know your rights if the puppy has a defect, because some defects affect the quality of a dog's life.

If you decide to buy from a pet store, ask around to make sure it has an excellent reputation. A good pet store is clean, the people who work there are knowledgeable, and its puppies are healthy.

Ask to see the registration application and health records for the puppy you want to buy before you put down a single penny. The name and address of the puppy's breeder are on the registration application form if you wish to check them out. Commercial breeders must have a license from the U.S. Department of Agriculture.

A Breeder or a Kennel

If you decide to purchase a purebred puppy, a good choice is to get him from someone who specializes in breeding only the type of dog you want. Many serious breeders specialize in one breed of dog and have lots of information

Choose a Breeder Carefully

A "breeder" is often someone who just produces a litter once in a while. This is the kind of breeder you usually find through friends or family members or in the classified ads. A breeder like this may not be familiar with the immunization and de-worming schedules the puppies need to follow. (See chapter 5 for more information on these health procedures.) Be sure to ask for and then check out references for anyone who has a puppy you're considering.

about it that they can share with you. They are the most qualified to give you information about that breed and what you can expect from it as an adult. Another advantage to buying from a breeder is that you'll probably be able to see the parents of the puppy.

Responsible breeders are able to answer almost any question you might have about a particular dog or the breed. They can guide you through the selection of the right puppy for you according to the puppy's temperament and your goals. Responsible breeders often ask you as many questions about yourself and your intentions for the puppy as you ask them about the puppy. This shows that they have an interest in where their dogs live.

Before You Buy a Puppy

Before you buy a puppy from anyone, ask about your guarantees. Tell the seller that you will take the puppy to your veterinarian the next day for a health check. Ask if you may return the puppy for a full refund if the health check isn't okay. Don't accept the answer, "You may have credit." If the puppy is sick with something contagious, all of their other puppies could be affected; you won't want another puppy from that place. Get the seller's policy on returning the puppy in writing. Do take the puppy to a veterinarian that day or the next day. Return the puppy if your veterinarian feels that he's not in good health or has a defect.

If you're buying a registered puppy, you should get a registration application from the kennel club that's registering it. This form must be made out from the breeder to the buyer. If the breeder sold the puppy to a pet store, for example, the registration application is transferred from the breeder to the pet store. The pet store must then attach a "transfer" slip showing that it's transferring the application to you. Don't accept any paperwork from a breeder to you, unless you're buying your puppy directly from the breeder. Paperwork must be correct or the puppy will be refused registration.

When at all possible pay for the puppy with a check or credit card. These may offer you more protection than a cash payment if the puppy is sick or defective and you find that the seller won't give you a refund when you return the puppy.

Checklist for Choosing a Healthy Puppy

Here are some things to look for to help you choose a healthy, well-adjusted puppy:

Temperament

Don't choose a puppy that is aggressive or one that is too shy. Look for a puppy that is curious, confident, and playful. Don't choose a fearful or withdrawn puppy because you feel sorry for him.

Structure

- Teeth: Check the way the teeth meet in the front of the mouth. In almost all breeds, the teeth should come together in a scissors bite, with the top teeth just barely overlapping the bottom teeth.

- Feet and legs: The feet should be compact and should point forward when the puppy is standing still. The hocks (comparable to our elbows) should point straight back, and not towards each other.

- If the puppy is a male, check to see if it has two testicles. If one or both of the testicles have not descended into the scrotum, castration surgery will be much more expensive.

Health Record

Ask for a full copy of the health record of any purebred puppy. It should show date of birth, sex, parents' names, breed, puppy identification number, and immunizations and de-worming schedules. You will need this for your veterinarian.

© KENT & DONNA DANNEN

Look for a puppy that is confident and friendly.

Consider Other Family Members

When you decide to add a dog to your life, it will be up to you to help other members of your family feel as comfortable as possible with your pet. Don't expect them to do your doggy chores because you have a ball game, are too tired or sick, or have grown bored with your pet. Some people just don't like touching animals. That's as much their right as it is your right to love them. Be sure that your dog doesn't get into their personal things or cause damage or a mess in their private areas. And be sure you always clean up after your dog in the yard or in the house.

Health

- Is the puppy's coat sleek and shiny, and free of fleas, ticks, and lice?

- Is the puppy the proper weight — not too thin or too fat?

- Are the skin and coat free of bare patches, scales, crusty places, and open sores?

- Are the ears clean and free of unpleasant odor?

- Are the eyes clear? Is the hair around the eyes unmatted?

- Is the puppy's feces formed instead of loose and runny, like diarrhea?

Records

Make sure you can get the following information from the person you get your puppy from:

- Date of birth.

- De-worming dates and product used.

- Types and dates of immunization already given and those still needed.

- For a purebred puppy, registration papers or pedigree.

- For a mixed-breed puppy, whatever information is available about his parents.

Getting Along with Other Animals in Your Family

If you already have animals in your family, you must think about how they will react to your new puppy or dog, and how the new member will react to them. A

Let dogs meet each other on neutral territory. Make sure both dogs are on leashes.

new puppy is usually accepted more readily than an older dog by dogs or animals that are already in the household. If you introduce an adult dog into a household that already has one or more adult dogs, there could be jealousy and even fights. The original dog(s) might "mark" the house and property with urine to show the newcomer that it's their territory. It's a good idea to introduce a new puppy or dog to a current family dog *away* from the home; otherwise, the resident dog may think the new dog is an intruder in his territory.

A nearby park that allows dogs could be the perfect place to arrange an introduction. Both dogs should be on leashes, held by two different people. Allow the dogs to greet each other in dog fashion. They will sniff and smell each other. If either dog shows aggression or undesirable behavior, the person holding the leash

Health Tip

Before you take your puppy to a public place that's used by other dogs, ask your veterinarian if it's safe. Some veterinarians recommend keeping puppies away from other dogs until they're about 16 weeks of age. By that time, a puppy's immune system can protect it from diseases that might be spread by other dogs.

should control the dog with a firm snap on the collar and a firm "no."

If the dogs greet each other in a friendly manner, allow them to interact and play together, keeping them under leash control. Let them work out who will be the "top dog." After this short introduction, you can take both dogs home. Be certain to give your original dog lots of attention, too, to avoid jealousy. Feeding should be in separate areas to avoid fighting.

If your family has animals other than dogs in the house or on the property, watch their attitude and that of the new puppy or dog. The puppy could be trampled by a cow or a goat, scratched by a cat, or kicked by a horse. A puppy doesn't realize his size or abilities and might try to chase the other animal.

Keep the new puppy or dog on a leash when he's introduced to new areas of the property and other animals, even in the house. If he's on a leash and exhibits a desire to chase, you can give him a leash correction and a firm "no." You won't have this kind of control over a dog that's running free and excited. Once the dog has learned the thrill of a chase, it isn't easy to change him.

Socializing and New Experiences

Introduce your puppy to a wide variety of experiences to build his confidence. New situations are stimulating. They help your puppy become well rounded and meet his potential. When you introduce your puppy to new situations, be alert to anything or anyone that might frighten him. Don't allow anyone to mishandle your pup, even unintentionally. To be on the safe side, don't let anyone pick up your puppy.

Introduce your dog to people and dogs of all types. Remember that some people are afraid of dogs and might not want to meet or pet your dog. Always ask permission of the owner of another dog before allowing the dogs to make contact. Then watch them very carefully to be sure there is no aggression on either dog's part.

A park or playground is a good place to take your puppy, but a very busy time there might be more than your young puppy can handle at first. Ease him into noisy or crowded situations gradually.

Be a good citizen when you take your dog to a public place. Always keep him under control and clean up after him.

CHAPTER

Your Dog's New Home

Dogs are pack animals — they like being part of a group. They're also very adaptable. A large majority of dogs would prefer to live with their owners. Not only would your dog like to live in your house, he would also like to sleep in your room. If you decided to move into the garage, barn, or backyard, he would be perfectly happy to move there with you. A dog that lives in the house learns more quickly because he is observing and interacting with people and their daily activities. He soon will learn what is acceptable behavior in your home, because you'll be there to direct him.

There are a few things to consider when you choose a place for your dog to live:

- A dog that lives inside your home needs to relieve himself several times a day, especially when he's young. If you or someone else cannot be available to walk your dog during the day, he will need an outside pen.

- Very small dogs or dogs with short hair coats shouldn't be kept outdoors if you live where the weather gets very cold.

- Puppies and older dogs may need extra protection from the weather.

If There's No Other Way

If there's no alternative, a dog that lives outside can be happy as long as you give him plenty of your time.

24

- Heavy-coated breeds and those with "pug" faces don't do well outside in very warm or very humid weather.

- Some puppies or dogs that are very active might need to have an outside area until they are trained to be less rambunctious in the house.

Indoor Accommodations

If your dog will have the privilege of living inside your home, he needs a comfortable place to rest and a place to eat.

Your Dog's Home in Your Home

The method I prefer for teaching dogs to live indoors is called crate training. (See chapter 6, pages 97–99, for more information on crate training.) The crate becomes your dog's home inside your house.

Pick a spot that will belong to your dog. That's where you'll place his crate. Choose a crate that's large enough for him to enter, turn around, and lie down comfortably. An airline crate works well, because it's lightweight and easy to wash and disinfect. The spot you choose should be in a relatively quiet place where the dog can go to rest. There should be good circulation of air around the crate, but it shouldn't be in the direct path of a heating or air-conditioning vent. The sun shouldn't shine directly on the crate, or the inside could get very hot.

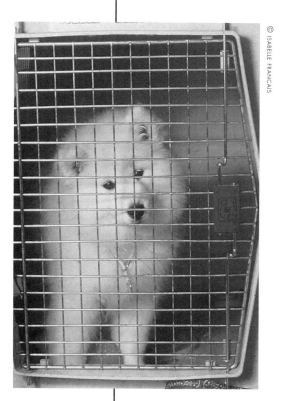

© ISABELLE FRANCAIS

An indoor dog should have a crate of his own.

A Crate Mat with a Removable Cover

Here's how to make a mat for your dog's crate so it will be more comfortable for sleeping.

For the cover, choose material that you like and that is both durable and washable. Canvas, denim, terry-cloth, and even fake sheepskin work well. Wash the fabric and dry it in the clothes dryer on "High." If the fabric is going to shrink, this will take care of it.

You will need:

- A piece of ¼-inch exterior masonite at least as large as the bottom of the crate
- Two rectangular pieces of fabric at least 12 inches longer on a side than the bottom of the crate
- Scissors
- Pinking shears (optional)
- Measuring tape or ruler
- Pencil or marker
- Straight pins
- Cardboard
- Strong thread

Make the Mat

1. Measure the inside bottom of the crate.

2. Ask someone to cut the masonite to the size of your measurements, and round off the corners as shown in the drawing.

3. Place the masonite in the crate to make sure it fits. If it doesn't, ask your carpenter to trim it so that it does fit.

Make the Cover

1. Add 12 inches to the length and width of your measurements for the bottom of the crate. If the crate measures 20 inches by 27 inches, the new measurements will be 32 inches by 39 inches.

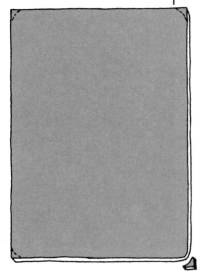

Ask someone to cut the masonite to size and round off the corners.

2. Cut two pieces of material to the measurements described above: the size of the bottom of the crate, plus 12 inches longer and wider. Try to use the selvages wherever possible to prevent raveling. Cut all other edges with pinking shears to prevent fraying during washing and drying.

3. On each piece of material, measure down 11¾ inches from one corner, and mark that place with a straight pin. On the diagram, that place is labeled A.

4. Measure 11¾ inches across the top from that corner, and mark the place with a straight pin. On the diagram, that place is labeled B.

5. Using a pencil or marker, draw a straight line from A to B, forming a triangle. Cut a piece of cardboard to exactly fit that triangle.

6. Keeping the cardboard in place in the corner of the fabric, fold it in half to find the middle of the line that forms the bottom of the triangle. Make a mark at this place, which is labeled C in the drawing.

7. Cut off each corner of the material, cutting along the line from A to B.

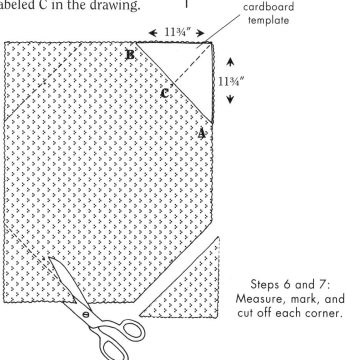

cardboard template

11¾"

11¾"

B

C

A

Steps 6 and 7: Measure, mark, and cut off each corner.

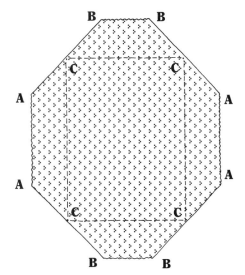

Your fabric will look like this when you've cut off all the corners.

8. Lay the material down flat with the right (outside) up. On the top and one side, fold the A and B flaps over so that their edges meet. Smooth out the material so there is a flat seam from the place where A and B meet to C. Sew this seam, reinforcing both the beginning and the end of the seam with backstitching. (Ask someone to show you how, if you need help.) That corner is done!

9. Repeat step 8 for each of the other three corners.

10. Turn the material inside out and fit the masonite into the cover, bending the masonite slightly as you slip it into the corner at the bottom and then the top of the cover.

11. Make the second cover following the same steps, and you have a spare!

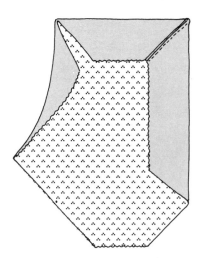

Steps 8 & 9: Fold the flaps over and sew the seams.

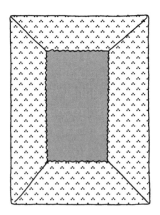

Step 10: Turn the material inside out and slip the masonite in.

Outdoor Accommodations

If your dog cannot live inside your house, he should have a pen of his own to keep him on your property. He should never be allowed to run free, no matter where you live — even in the country.

If your dog lives outside, you must be a responsible owner. Remember that your neighbors' right to peace, quiet, and privacy must not be violated by your dog.

The Pen

A pen in the yard should give your dog enough room to exercise. A square pen is better than a rectangular one, because it seems to control the "running the fence" syndrome — when the dog runs back and forth along the long side of the fence. The sides should be wire mesh of a type that the dog cannot climb. The fence should be high enough so that the dog can't jump out. Solid material is a good idea for fences that you share with neighbors, to prevent your dog from interfering with their activities.

Shelter

There should be plenty of shade in the pen, so your dog can get out of the sun at all hours of the day. Provide a dog-house or dog igloo with the opening facing a direction that will protect it from cold winds. The roof of the dog house shouldn't be flat, unless you place it in the pen so that the dog can't use it as a step for jumping over the fence.

If you live in an area where the climate gets very cold in winter, you might wish to insulate the dog-house. The house or igloo should also be set up on

Helpful Hint

The ground surface of the pen should be of concrete or a gravel mixture. Unless it's very large, a dog pen that has only grass and dirt can become a mud hole when it rains.

Fences should be of a material your dog can't climb.

Doggy Door

If you have a fenced yard and would like your dog to have access to it from inside, you might think about a doggy door. Try to get one that can't be blown open by the wind and that can be closed off to prevent entry from inside and out. This helps in bad weather, when you might want to prevent your dog from getting muddy or wet and then messing up your house.

blocks or rails in a high part of the pen so that it will never be sitting in water.

Outdoor Toys

Provide some safe playthings appropriate for the size and temperament of your particular dog. Small garden-tractor or lawn-mower tires are a great toy for medium to large breeds. Hard-rubber toys make durable outside playthings. However, many dogs won't play with toys if they're alone.

Most puppies and dogs quickly learn to use a doggy door.

Never Chain or Tie Out Your Dog

A chain and tie-out cable are two things you won't need on your list. The only time a dog should be attached to a line is when you're with him and he's on a leash.

A social animal such as a dog that's tied up for the major portion of his life can become aggressive, and is almost always hyperactive when he is released. These dogs are difficult to control and train. Every other living thing that they see from the end of their chain is free to come and go, walk and run. When they are loose, they try to make up for lost time.

It's a very good idea, however, to teach your dog to accept being tied for short lengths of time, with you present. You may find yourself in a situation where you're out with your dog, you don't have his crate along, and you need to restrain him. If you have taught your dog to "stay" while being tied, without straining on his leash, this may prove to be helpful to you.

Never leave your dog when he is tied. Always use a buckle collar that fits snugly and won't slip over his head. Don't use a slip collar.

Food and Water

You will need to choose a place for your new dog's food and water. It's also important to have the right dishes for food and water.

Choose a Place

Pick an area where you can put a small mat for your dog's food and water dishes. Feed your dog in the same place, every day. I don't suggest feeding your dog in the crate unless you have more than one animal and they fight over the food. Even in this instance, try to find

Danger!

Dogs that are tied, cabled, or chained can get tangled up and injure themselves. They can even die from choking or hanging.

A Bad Idea

Have you ever heard a city person say, "I'm looking for a home for my dog in the country where he can run free"? This is a bad idea. No matter where they live, dogs running loose can get into all kinds of trouble:

- Digging up the neighbor's garden
- Chasing or killing livestock
- Mating with other dogs
- Running into traffic
- In most places it's not legal for dogs to run loose, and it's *never* right for owners to let them.

another way of solving the problem. For an outside dog, food and water dishes should be placed where they won't get direct sun. Algae grows fast in water that receives direct sunlight, and sunlight causes wet food to spoil. Both can make your dog sick.

Food and Water Containers

It's best to buy dishes made especially for dogs. Many containers you find around the house, barn, or shop are not suitable or safe to serve your dog's food or water in. They may have held dangerous poisons, fuels, fertilizers, pesticides, baits, paints, or other chemicals that can never be completely washed out. Some crockery made outside the United States is treated with lead at one stage of the processing. These can all be harmful to your dog, and also to you.

Food and water dishes for dogs are available in a great variety of styles, materials, colors, and sizes.

Stainless steel. Dishes made of stainless steel are easy to wash and sanitize and are virtually indestructible. A problem with stainless steel, however, is that it's lightweight and can easily be pushed around by your dog. One style has a rubber strip along the outer edge on the bottom that prevents the bowl from sliding.

Crockery. Glazed crockery dishes are easy to wash and sanitize. They are heavy and usually have a rough bottom that makes the bowl skidproof. However, they can break if dropped on a hard surface.

Pails and Buckets

You could use a pail or bucket to provide water for your dog. Use a clip on its handle to attach it to a permanent structure. Stainless-steel buckets are available in sizes from 1 to 32 quarts. Heavy plastic or rubber buckets can work for large dogs, but are usually not available in sizes suitable for small or toy breeds.

Choose a dish that is the right size for your dog and that is easy to sanitize.

Plastic. Plastic bowls come in many bright colors. The thickness and quality of the plastic can vary widely. Some bowls are made of very thick, high-quality material and resemble crockery dishes. They are easy to wash but eventually develop scratches, making it harder to sanitize them. The thinner plastic dishes are lightweight and therefore easily destroyed by chewing dogs.

Choose dishes that are made of a durable material that's easy to clean, and that will hold enough food for one meal and enough water for one day.

Puppy Proofing

Look around your house and your yard or anyplace your puppy will be able to go. Look from your standing level, then get down on the ground and look at the area from a puppy's point of view. Look for things your puppy might chew or swallow, knock over, or get tangled in. Read the section on preventing accidents on pages 85–86.

Keep Those Ears Clean!

The very long ears of dogs such as Basset Hounds or Bloodhounds may get in their food when they eat. They can then smear it on themselves and on your furniture, carpet, and clothing. Dirty ears can develop skin problems. They can also attract flies and other insects. If you have a long-eared dog, you might want to get a special bowl that's very tall and narrow at the top. When the dog's muzzle is in this bowl, his ears will fall out on either side and stay clean.

Feeding Your Dog

Every one of our pet dogs today descended from wild dogs that hunted for their meals. They lived primarily on other mammals and birds. Because the wild dogs hunted other animals, you might think their diet was all meat. This wasn't the case. Most of the animals that they hunted ate grasses, shrubs, and other plants. The wild dogs ate not only the meat and fat of their prey, but also the contents of their prey's stomach and intestines. This partially digested plant matter and the enzymes it contained were important elements of the wild dogs' diet.

Wild dogs also ate certain organs, such as the liver and kidneys. When they a cleaned the carcass, they gnawed the bones. When prey was scarce, wild dogs would eat the remains of animals killed by other predators, or they would eat fruits, nuts, and other plant matter.

Our pet dogs today require the same nutrients that their wild ancestors did. The levels of some of the basic elements have changed because of lifestyle changes as dogs have evolved from wild to domestic animals. Even though most pet dogs today don't have the same energy requirements that their very active wild dog ancestors did, you should give careful thought to what you feed your dog. With good nutrition, he has the best opportunity to grow properly and stay healthy.

Survival Skill

In order to survive, the ancestors of our pet dogs had to be able to change their eating habits when necessary.

Necessary Nutrients

The components that are absolutely essential in a dog's diet are water, carbohydrates, fats, protein, vitamins, minerals, and fiber. Dog foods are labeled with the percentage of each of these ingredients, as well as of *ash*. (See page 37 for more information about ash.)

Water

The bodies of living animals and plants are made up mostly of water. Dogs are not able to store extra water in their bodies, so they must obtain it from the foods they eat or by drinking it. Water helps regulate a dog's body temperature and flush out waste products.

Every dog needs clean, fresh water at all times. It's critically important for any dog that eats dry dog food as the main part of its diet, to prevent severe digestive upsets that could even result in death.

Carbohydrates

Energy your dog needs to be active and grow comes from carbohydrates, as well as from fats and protein. Carbohydrates are found in grains and other plant sources. To be most helpful to your dog, carbohydrates should be fed in cooked form. Commercial dog foods contain cooked carbohydrates as a low-cost source of energy.

Fats

Fat is a very concentrated energy source that contains important fatty acids. Along with protein, it makes dog food taste good to your dog. The right amount of fat will help keep his skin and coat healthy and in good condition. Very active dogs can eat a diet higher in fat than inactive dogs, but a diet with too much fat or carbohydrates will cause most dogs to gain too much weight.

Dog food labels tell you what's inside.

Thirsty!

Your dog will drink more water when he has been active, when the weather is warm or hot, and when he has eaten dry dog food or salty snacks. Your dog may also need a lot of water when he's sick.

Protein

Protein is found in meats, meat by-products, some vegetables, grains, and nuts. It's another source of energy, and important for muscle, hair, and bone growth and repair. Meat protein is probably the most important ingredient for making dog food tasty to your dog. A dog that doesn't get enough protein in his food can experience poor growth, dull hair coat, susceptibility to diseases, and poor healing. Protein is the most expensive part of dog food.

Vitamins

Vitamin Danger
Too much of certain vitamins can cause health problems in dogs, so adding vitamins to your dog's regular dog food isn't a good idea without your veterinarian's advice.

Vitamins are nutrients your dog needs to grow properly, be active, and resist diseases. Vitamins are found in many dog foods, as long as the foods have been properly packaged and stored. Dry foods should be stored in airtight containers and protected from high temperatures. Good commercial dog foods contain the vitamins that occur naturally in their ingredients along with some that are added to bring the vitamin content up to the level that dogs need.

Minerals and Trace Elements

Minerals and trace elements are natural substances and chemicals that are necessary in a dog's diet. They must be included in the diet in balanced amounts. Some work together with others in specific amounts; too much of one or too little of another can cause serious health problems. Manufacturers of good commercial dog foods perform laboratory tests on their products to make sure that the minerals are in proper balance. You shouldn't add minerals to your dog's diet without specific instructions from your veterinarian.

Fiber

Fiber is also called roughage. Your dog needs fiber in his diet as an aid in digestion and to provide the bulk that helps wastes move through his digestive system. Too little fiber may cause constipation. A dog whose diet contains too much fiber produces a larger volume of stool material, because there's less digestible material in his food. Special dog foods for dogs on weight-loss diets are higher in fiber.

Ash

When anything is burned, organic matter is consumed, leaving only a residue. This is called ash and is composed of inorganic materials, including minerals. Dog food labels tell how much ash the food contains.

Plan Your Feeding Program

You will want to feed your dog properly to keep him healthy, happy, active, and satisfied. But there's more to it than just buying any dog food and feeding him once or twice a day. Dog foods differ in quality, nutritional value, appearance, price, and taste. You will want to buy the best dog food available for the price your family can afford.

Deciding what and how much to feed is a complex subject. Individual dogs have specific nutritional requirements, depending on several factors.

Buy the best dog food your family can afford.

Is Your Dog a Puppy?

Puppies are very active and have good appetites. This is the best time to help them form good eating habits.

A puppy's skeleton grows to its approximate adult height by 9 to 18 months of age, depending on the breed. A puppy needs food with the proper proportions of nutrients, so that they can be easily converted to muscle and bone, and also provide for a puppy's boundless energy. Special foods that are formulated for puppies contain these ingredients, as well as the proper ratio of vitamin and mineral supplements.

Sadie's dishes won't tip over easily because they have wide, flat bottoms.

Size	Adult Weight	Examples	Mature Age
Toy	Under 10 lbs.	Chihuahua, Pekinese	6 mos.
Small	10–20 lbs.	Dachshund, Boston Terrier	9 mos.
Medium	20–50 lbs.	Beagle, Miniature Schnauzer	10–15 mos.
Large	50–100 lbs.	Dalmatian, Retrievers	18 mos.
Giant	Over 100 lbs.	Great Dane, Rottweiler	Over 20 mos.

Smaller breeds reach maturity sooner than larger breeds.

How Big Will Your Puppy Be as an Adult?

An adult dog is one that has reached maturity and has grown to his full adult height. He can continue to add muscle, but doesn't need the same level of certain minerals and other nutrients that puppies do.

The smaller dog breeds reach adult size at a younger age than the giant dog breeds. Depending on the kind of dog you have, the chart above might give you an idea of when your puppy will reach maturity and how much he will weigh.

Does Your Dog Have Special Nutritional Needs?

Dogs with certain traits and allergies may require nutrients at levels different from those an average dog needs. Allergic dogs may even need dog foods that contain substitutions for the types of meats and grains found in most dog foods. They may need to be fed a hypoallergenic diet containing lamb and rice, for example, instead of beef or chicken and wheat or corn.

How Active Is Your Dog?

Dogs that work or play hard need more energy from their food than dogs that are less active. Dogs confined to a house or a small pen may not have the opportunity to be very active. If you feed high-energy foods to an inactive dog, he will become overweight and develop serious health problems related to his excess fat.

What's the Health, Age, and Condition of Your Dog?

Younger dogs need more food per pound of body weight than older dogs of the same weight. Older dogs need less fat in their diet than younger dogs. Old dogs can benefit from special "senior maintenance" foods that also contain reduced protein.

Obese dogs should have a diet with reduced fat content. This could be accomplished by cutting down on the amount of food the dog is given, but he may still feel hungry. Special foods have been formulated for these dogs that are high in volume and low in fat. The dogs can be fed the normal amount, but they won't be getting as many calories.

There are specially formulated diets available from your veterinarian for dogs that have allergies; malnutrition; diabetes; diseases of the kidney, liver, heart, and digestive tract; as well as other health problems.

What's the Climate Where You Live?

Dogs that live outside or spend a great deal of time outdoors have greater energy requirements during certain times of the year. They need to build and maintain an insulating layer of fat if they are outside during cold weather. Because of this, you could feed them a higher-fat diet prior to the onset of cold weather, so that their bodies can prepare the

Pregnant Dogs Have Special Needs

A female that's pregnant or nursing puppies has very special nutritional requirements to supplement her body and the growing babies.

insulating layer. The fat in their diet should be decreased as the weather warms.

Dogs that are fat during hot weather have a difficult time keeping cool. Normal panting, which helps regulate body temperature, may not be as effective for a dog if he's fat.

How Often Should You Feed Your Dog?

A puppy needs to be fed more often than an adult dog. He needs more food than an adult of the same weight, but his stomach is small. That's why you will need to feed a puppy several small meals a day to make up the quantity needed.

When you buy your puppy or dog, ask what schedule has been used to feed him. Very young puppies of 6 to 10 weeks may be fed as often as three times a day. Older puppies are gradually changed to twice a day. Adult dogs can be fed two small meals or one larger meal per day. Aging dogs that are not able to eat one large meal a day could be fed two small meals instead.

It's very important that you feed your dog at about the same time each day. Dogs like routine in their lives. They can become upset if a meal is late.

How Much Should You Feed Your Dog?

Commercial dog foods are specifically made for different-aged dogs. There's usually a suggested feeding schedule on the container, depending on the size of the dog. This doesn't take into consideration the activity level of your dog or the climatic conditions, however. This basic schedule is correct for an average, moderately active dog in moderate climatic conditions; but if your dog is outside in cold weather, is extremely active, or both, the amount of food should be increased. It's difficult to give an exact amount, because foods vary in

What about Free-Choice Feeding?

Keeping dry food available to your dog at all times might be convenient for you, but it may create some problems. Your dog may become a picky eater, or he may overeat and get fat. Rodents and insects will be attracted to the food. They can introduce diseases and parasites to your dog. Dog food that gets wet can rapidly spoil and make your dog sick.

composition and weight. A cup of pelleted dry dog food weighs much more than a cup of expanded dry dog food, because the pelleted food is more dense. The same rule applies to other forms of dog foods, such as canned or semimoist types.

Establishing Good Eating Habits

It's easy to start a puppy off on the right paw by using proper feeding methods that promote good eating habits. Feed your puppy at regular times every day, in the same place and using the same dish. Feed an appropriate, well-balanced dog food. If the puppy is very young he may need the food moistened with warm water. Pick up any uneaten food after 30 minutes. Have fresh water available at all times. In a very short time, your puppy will learn the schedule. He will learn that he cannot play during feeding time, or the food will disappear and he will still be hungry.

Never feed your dog tidbits from your dinner table or from your kitchen counter. Doing so even once can permanently train your dog to beg for human foods. Your dog could begin to refuse his regular dog food and beg or pine away for Mom's or Dad's home cooking. Family mealtime could become unpleasant with incessant whining or begging.

It is hard to throw away leftovers when you have a dog looking at you with pleading eyes and saliva dripping from his jaws. Some leftovers — those that are healthful and low in fat — can be added occasionally in small amounts to your dog's regular dog food at the regular time. Just remember that he will look forward to and expect this delicious addition to his diet whenever the smell of cooking fills the air. And remember that too much human food isn't good for your dog's health.

Ingredients versus Nutrients

All dog food labels must have a listing of the ingredients. The ingredients are listed in the order of the volume in which they're found in the dog food. If the food contains more corn products than anything else, then "corn products" is listed first. If your dog has an allergy to one of the ingredients, you can avoid that food.

Choosing Your Dog's Food

Dog foods are available in a variety of consistencies, shapes, textures, and flavors. What appeals to you and is most attractive to your dog is not necessarily the best choice for his regular diet.

Homemade Diets

Some people think their dog's diet would be more nutritious if they prepared the food from scratch at home. In reality this is very often not the case. A dog's nutrition is very complex. It takes a thorough understanding of a particular dog's nutritional needs to arrive at the proper balance of ingredients.

All foods in a homemade diet for dogs should be thoroughly cooked. Raw meats can contain harmful bacteria, which cooking will destroy. Vegetable matter is more digestible for dogs when it has been cooked.

Feeding Tip

Dogs prefer their moist meals warm or at room temperature. Most dogs don't like cold or frozen food.

When it comes to your dog's food, there are plenty of choices.

Vitamin and mineral supplements should probably be added, but it's difficult to know the exact amount of each to add. The types of meats appropriate for this type of diet may make the dog food very expensive. Less costly meat and meat by-products may have a high fat content. Some meat by-products have a strong odor. For all of these reasons, I recommend that you use a good commercial dog food.

Canned Dog Food

Water is the main ingredient of canned food, often up to 80 percent of its total weight. Canned food is often mixed with dry food and a little water to stimulate a dog's appetite.

This type of food comes in cans of various sizes, from 5-ounce single portions for small dogs to 64-ounce containers. Once the can is opened, any unused food must be covered and refrigerated.

Canned foods may be 100 percent meat, but most brands have lower proportions of meat to other ingredients. Look at the label. If it says "100% horsemeat," it must be 100 percent horsemeat. If the label says "chicken dinner," 25 percent of the total weight of the solids must be derived from chicken or chicken by-products. If the label says "liver flavored dinner" or "chunks," there is less than 25 percent of liver or liver by-products in the solids.

Canned foods are lower in fiber and more digestible than dry foods. Vitamin supplements are added to replace those lost in cooking.

Semimoist Dog Food

Semimoist dog foods are available in pelleted form and in pieces that look like raw hamburger patties or chunks of ham. This is a product that looks appealing to the dog's owner. The dog doesn't care how it looks — only about how it smells and tastes.

Semimoist foods can contain up to 40 percent water, along with various ingredients to stop the growth of bacteria and molds and to keep the food from drying out. Once opened, packages must be refrigerated. Semimoist foods are very digestible.

Dry Dog Food

Dry dog food comes in boxes or bags of from 2 to 50 pounds. The individual pieces are a vast array of flavors, shapes, and colors. Some varieties have both crunchy and semimoist pieces in the same bag. Some varieties are flavor coated. Some have several shapes, colors, and flavors all in the same bag. Some have color added so that the food will appeal to the dog's owner. The dog doesn't care about the color or shape of her food.

Some dog owners moisten dry food with warm water prior to serving it to the dog. This releases the aroma and makes eating a little easier. Crunchy dry dog food can help keep a dog's teeth cleaner, however.

Refrigerated or Frozen Dog Food

These dog foods usually are found only at pet stores, kennels, and dog shows. One type of food comes in a long roll like bologna. It's sliced and fed as a training treat or broken up and mixed with regular dry dog food and a little warm water. Once opened, it must be refrigerated.

Frozen dog foods can be a combination of ground meats, ingredients found in dry dog foods, and water. They are very digestible, but may be too high in protein to be fed as a dog's total diet. They're excellent when mixed with dry food and water. Some types can be compressed into little balls to serve as training treats.

Health Warning

You may find frozen or refrigerated meat or meat parts in your supermarket labeled "food for dogs." If you don't know the source of the raw meat, be sure to cook it. Always wash your hands with soap after you handle raw meat. If you don't, the bacteria from the raw meat could make you sick.

Supplements

You don't have to add vitamin and mineral supplements to your dog's diet if you are feeding a good-quality commercial dog food; this has already been done by the manufacturer. In fact, an excess of certain vitamins and minerals, or those fed in the incorrect proportions or combinations, can cause a serious nutritional imbalance. Supplement only upon the recommendation of your veterinarian. If your dog isn't overweight, however, and you want to add a little shine to his coat, you can add 1 teaspoon to 2 tablespoons of corn oil to his daily ration. The amount would depend on your dog's weight.

Treats and Snacks

There are hundreds of varieties of dog treats and snacks for sale in stores. Many of them are made to appeal to a dog's owner. The dog really doesn't care what they look like. He cares about how the snack tastes. There are treats for long-term chewing satisfaction. (See pages 122–124 for information on chew treats.) There are also edible treats such as bone-shaped biscuits, hot dogs, pepperoni, jerky, steaks, hamburgers, cookies, dog "chocolate" candy, and

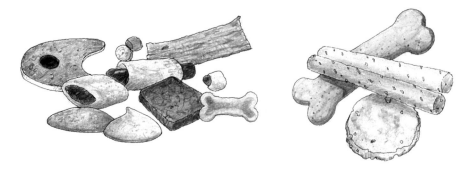

Your dog doesn't care what a treat looks like — only how it tastes.

edible chewing treats. These items come in proportions for dogs of all sizes. Most treats are very high in fat content and can contribute to obesity if you give your dog too many.

Recipes for Homemade Dog Treats

You can bake healthy treats for your dog in your own kitchen. Ask your parents if you can save leftover meat scraps. Cut them into very tiny pieces and store them in a bag or container in the freezer. When you have about 2 cups saved, they can be dried on a cookie sheet in the oven and added to some of the recipes below.

To dry, place the cut-up meat on a cookie sheet in the oven at about 250°F for about 30 to 45 minutes. Remove from the oven and let cool. What you don't use in a recipe can be saved in the freezer.

Oatmeal Dog Cookies

1½ cups whole wheat flour
1½ cups oatmeal
½ cup dried meat chips
¼ cup wheat germ

½ cup nonfat instant milk powder
¼ cup corn oil
2 tablespoons molasses
½ cup warm water

1. Preheat your oven to 300°F.

2. Mix the dry ingredients well and add the liquids, stirring until well blended.

3. Drop by teaspoons onto a greased cookie sheet. Flatten with floured fingers or a fork.

4. Bake in the preheated oven for 1 hour.

Ball Park Wieners

2 cups whole wheat flour
½ cup whole grain cereal
2 tablespoons bonemeal
½ cup nonfat dry milk powder
½ teaspoon garlic powder

½ cup corn oil
1 egg
½ cup water
1 beaten egg
Red and yellow food coloring

1. Preheat your oven to 350°F.

2. Combine all of the ingredients except the beaten egg, water, and food coloring. Add enough water to make a dough that won't stick to your hands.

3. Divide into three parts.

4. Add a few drops of red food coloring to one part and knead until it is uniformly red.

5. Wash your hands to remove any coloring.

6. Take about one-quarter of one of the remaining two pieces and knead in a few drops of yellow food coloring until the dough is uniformly bright yellow, like mustard.

7. Wash your hands to remove any coloring.

8. Take all the rest of the uncolored dough and knead together.

9. Divide into 12 pieces if you have a large dog, or 24 pieces if you have a small dog.

10. Pat each piece out into an oval about twice as long as it is wide and about ¼ inch thick, to form the bun.

11. Divide the red dough into the same number of pieces, and roll into hot dog shapes about the same length as the first dough pieces are long. Place each in the middle of a bun.

12. Wash your hands.

13. Roll or pat the yellow dough into a piece about ⅛ inch thick.

14. Cut with a butter knife into long, narrow, curvy strips to resemble mustard.

15. Brush the hot dog with the beaten egg and place the mustard on top.

16. Roll the sides of the bun over the hot dog and mustard and place on a greased cookie sheet.

17. Bake in the preheated oven until hard (30 to 45 minutes).

18. Check to see if the rolls are hard. If they're baked but not hard, turn off the oven and leave the pan inside until the oven is cool.

19. Remove the rolls from the oven, cool, and store in an airtight jar or bag in the refrigerator or freezer.

Whole Grain Dog Biscuits

2 bouillon cubes dissolved
1½ cups warm water
2 eggs
1 cup shredded cheese
2½ cups whole grain flours
  (your choice)

1 cup wheat germ
1 cup cornmeal
1 cup whole rolled oats
1 teaspoon garlic powder
½ cup instant nonfat milk
  powder

1. Preheat your oven to 300°F.

2. Dissolve the bouillon cubes in the water.

3. When dissolved, add eggs and cheese and mix thoroughly.

4. Add 1½ cups of the whole grain flour and all of the other ingredients. Mix thoroughly.

5. Add just enough more of the whole grain flour to make a dough that you can roll out ¼ inch thick.

6. Cut with cookie cutters and place on a lightly greased cookie sheet.

7. Bake in the preheated oven for 1 hour.

8. Turn off the oven. Turn the biscuits over and let them sit in the hot oven for 2 more hours or overnight to dry. Biscuits that won't be used within a week or two should be refrigerated in a moisture-proof bag.

Cut-Out Dog Cookies

3 cups whole wheat flour
1–2 cups alfalfa leaves from baled
    hay, or chopped fresh parsley
½ cup dry milk powder
1 teaspoon sugar
1 teaspoon trace mineral salt

½ cup corn oil
½ cup of meaty dog food
    (pureed in a blender)
1 egg
Water

1. Preheat your oven to 350°F.

2. Mix all the ingredients with enough water to make a dough that won't stick to your hands.

3. Roll or pat the dough to about ½ inch thick.

4. Cut into shapes with cookie cutters.

5. Bake on a greased cookie sheet for 30 minutes or until hard.

Dog Pretzels

1 package active dry yeast
⅔ cup warm water
1 teaspoon sugar
1 cup whole wheat flour
4 tablespoons wheat germ
2 tablespoons bonemeal

½ cup nonfat instant milk powder
1 teaspoon trace mineral salt
2 tablespoons corn oil
1 beaten egg
Whole grain or rolled grain
    cereal

1. Dissolve the yeast in the warm water and add the sugar.

2. Combine the dry ingredients and add the yeast mixture.

3. Knead until smooth.

4. Place dough in a lightly oiled bowl and let rise in a warm place until doubled.

5. Punch down the dough and divide it into pieces about the size of a golf ball.

6. Roll each piece into a rope and shape into pretzels or other designs, such as hearts, spirals, and so on.

7. Place the treats on an oiled cookie sheet and let them rise until doubled.

8. Preheat your oven to 375°F. Bake the treats for 15 minutes.

9. Remove from the oven. Glaze with the beaten egg and garnish with the whole or rolled grain.

10. Bake another 20 minutes or until hard.

Dog-Newtons

3 cups whole wheat flour
½ cup brewer's yeast
   (found at pet stores)
1 cup cracked whole grain
   cereal
½ cup cornmeal
½ cup corn oil

½ cup nonfat instant milk
   powder
2 teaspoons baking powder
1 egg
1–1½ cups soup stock (or water)
1 cup of meaty dog food
   (pureed in a blender)

1. Preheat your oven to 300°F.

2. Blend all of the ingredients except the soup stock (or water) and the pureed dog food in a bowl.

3. Add enough of the soup stock to make a mixture you can handle without getting your hands sticky.

4. Divide the dough in half.

5. Grease a jelly roll pan and roll out half of the dough to fit the bottom of the pan.

6. Spread the dog food puree over the dough.

7. Take the remaining dough and roll it out to fit the top of the jelly roll pan.

8. Place it on top of the puree and pat it down with your hands. Seal the edges so the puree won't leak out.

9. Bake in the preheated oven for 45 minutes.

10. Remove from the oven. While it's still warm, cut into portions according to the size of your dog.

11. Shut off the oven and return the pan to the oven for the treats to harden, about 2 hours.

12. Remove from the oven. When the treats are cool, place them in plastic bags and refrigerate or freeze.

CHAPTER 4

Grooming

Your own body feels refreshed after you've taken a shower, especially if you've scrubbed your skin with a rough washcloth or a scrub puff. Your body tingles and you feel lively. You look clean and you smell good, too.

Your dog feels the same way after you groom him. Watch your dog after you've bathed and brushed him. He will jump and run and feel frisky. He loves being clean. Your dog is telling you, "Thank you, thank you!"

Grooming includes bathing, brushing, combing, trimming nails, cleaning ears, checking and cleaning teeth, and checking anal glands. Dogs with medium and long coats need brushing and combing more frequently than dogs with short coats.

Before You Bathe or Groom Your Puppy

Prepare your puppy for grooming by introducing him to the brush or comb when you're in the middle of a playing session. Don't treat the brush as a toy, however. This is also a good time for the puppy to get used to your handling every square inch of his body. He already loves to be petted and stroked, so it probably won't be long before you can pet and stroke him with the brush or comb. Don't rush it, though. Take as much time as your puppy needs to feel comfortable.

Reasons for Grooming Your Dog

- Helps to stimulate and condition your dog's body, skin, and coat.

- Gives you a chance to find fleas, ticks, burrs, and hidden injuries.

- Gives you a chance to check and maintain nails, teeth, and ears.

- Reduces shedding.

- Gives your dog your extra time and attention.

Use the back of the brush if the puppy seems resistant to the bristles. When he accepts soft brushing with the bristles, gradually brush with a little more pressure until you can brush or comb all the way to the skin. Brush or comb all parts of the puppy, including his ears, face, and feet.

Bathing

There's no exact rule for how often to bathe your dog. Normally, dogs that live inside need bathing more frequently than dogs that live outside. Every two months is usually adequate to keep a dog from spreading dirt and odors around the house. No matter where the dog lives, though, if he is dirty or starts to get that "doggy" smell, it's time for a bath. Some breeds develop a strong doggy odor sooner than others, and this odor can cling to carpets, furniture, clothing, and even people. Remember, however, that frequent bathing can remove the natural oils that condition a dog's hair. If you must bathe your dog often, you may need to use skin and coat conditioners to prevent dry skin and brittle hair.

Shampoos and Conditioners

Shopping for dog shampoo can be quite confusing. Shampoos are available for a variety of purposes. Flea-and-tick shampoo kills these pests as the dog is bathed. Tearless shampoo is mild and reduces eye irritation. Tar-medicated shampoo is for dogs with skin allergies caused by fleas or skin inflammation. Medicated shampoo treats dry, itchy skin caused by allergies. Protein shampoo conditions and doesn't remove natural oils from the hair. Extra-body shampoo improves the hair texture in breeds that have *double coats*.

Avoid a Chill

Very young puppies and sick dogs could get chilled during a bath and shouldn't be bathed unless it's absolutely necessary. If you absolutely must bathe a very young puppy, make sure you keep him warm during and after the bath.

Muddy Dog Treatment

If your dog gets muddy and you don't want to bathe him right away, try this: Wait until his hair is dry. Then brush the hair vigorously in both directions to loosen the dried mud. Follow up by wiping the dog's coat with a damp towel.

For the average dog, a flea-and-tick shampoo would be your best choice if you live in an area of the country where these pests are a problem. A tearless shampoo is your best choice in other areas.

Coat conditioners, creme rinses, and oils are available to moisturize dry skin or coat, to detangle, and to add luster. Some conditioners and most rinses are applied after the dog has been bathed and rinsed. Other conditioners are not rinsed out. Be sure to read the label directions on the product you choose. Remember that detanglers and conditioners are not meant to replace routine combing and brushing.

Your Puppy's First Bath

The water, brushes, combs, and soaps that go along with grooming could scare a puppy that has never been groomed or hasn't been groomed properly. It's important for you to make grooming a positive experience for you and your dog. If you lose his trust the first time, you may have a very hard time winning it back.

Ask someone to help you the first few times you bathe your puppy. For the first bath, use a tub with only a few inches of lukewarm water.

Put your puppy into the tub and have your helper squat down in front of him, holding his collar on both sides.

Let the puppy get used to the tub and water for a minute or so. Praise the puppy if he remains calm.

Place a cotton ball that you've lightly dipped in mineral oil in each ear. Use an eyedropper to place one or two drops of mineral oil into each eye.

Slowly scoop up some of the warm water from the tub with a cup and pour it over the puppy's shoulders. Praise him if he remains calm. Repeat this until he's completely wet.

Talk quietly to your puppy. It doesn't matter what you say, only how you say it. Every few sentences throw in something like, "You're a very good dog today."

Equipment for Bathing

- Collar and leash
- Tearless shampoo
- Conditioner (if needed)
- Combs and brushes
- Mineral oil
- Plastic cup
- Eyedropper
- Washing brush or mitt (optional)
- Cotton balls
- Washcloth
- Towels
- Tub
- Flea-and-tick dip or spray

Gather all the things you'll need for your puppy's bath before you start.
A buckle collar helps you control the puppy during the bath.

Apply water to your puppy's face with your hand. Don't let any soap get into his eyes or nose.

Apply a line of tearless shampoo down the middle of the puppy's back, from between his ears to the base of his tail. Rub this in thoroughly with a mitt or your fingers. Scrub gently at first. Increase the pressure if the puppy is receptive. Pour a small amount of water over him and scrub to make a richer lather.

Check your puppy's ears, tail, face, and feet for dirt, seeds, and ticks. Look in the little pocket at the outside edge of the ear, near the head. Clean this area with a washcloth. Check between each toe and under the tail.

Bathtub Ideas

If you bathe your puppy outdoors, you can use a small child's wading pool or a disposable mortar box as a bathtub. Mortar boxes are available at builders' supply stores.

Vinegar Rinse

Use a vinegar rinse to reduce flaking and static electricity if your dog has dry skin.

- 1 ounce white vinegar
- 1 quart warm water

Mix together and apply to your freshly shampooed and rinsed dog. Leave the rinse on for about 10 minutes. Make sure your dog doesn't get chilled during this time. Place him in his crate or, on a warm day, take him for a walk. After the 10 minutes, rinse thoroughly again.

Bathing your dog can be fun for you, your dog, and a friend.

Check around the eyes and ears for seeds. Some seeds have little hooks that work into fur; others have a sticky substance.

Be sure to scrub the feet, the chest, and under the tail.

When you're finished, rinse the puppy thoroughly. Use a hose if you're outside, working from the rump forward, against the direction of the hair's growth. If you're inside, use a plastic cup or tumbler to pour clean water over the puppy. Run your fingers through the coat, separating the hairs to see if there's any soap left. If you see any, keep rinsing.

If your puppy's skin or coat is dry, you might wish to apply a conditioner or even a vinegar rinse.

After a Bath

Rub your puppy with a towel to get him as dry as possible. You might try using a hair dryer, but be sure it's set on cool.

You can brush and comb your puppy while you're drying him. If he has a long coat, don't pull on any stubborn matted or tangled patches, because that will hurt him. Remember, you want this to be a pleasant

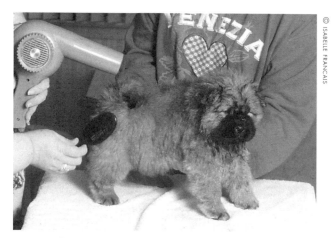

A hair dryer might frighten a puppy at first.

Be Careful!
Never use a hair dryer anywhere near water!

experience. Use a spray-on tangle remover with or without a *mat splitter*. You can also cut out mats that are small.

If you put your puppy in his crate to dry instead of using a hair dryer, drying will take longer and he might get cold. Don't let him run and play outside, even if it's a nice day. His natural instinct will be to roll in the dirt, and you'll have to start all over.

When the puppy is dry after his bath, brush or comb his hair again. This will stimulate the skin and distribute the coat's natural oils. It will also help prevent mats and tangles in long-coated dogs.

Brushing and Combing

Dog breeds differ in the lengths and textures of their coats. Many breeds shed a small amount of hair every day, and shed profusely twice a year. Brushing and combing can help reduce the amount of hair shed in the house. Most long-coated breeds should be brushed at least once or twice a week. Breeds with very heavy coats or very fine long hair must be brushed every day.

Flea Shampoo

If your dog has fleas, you can make your own flea shampoo.

- 1 20-ounce bottle generic baby shampoo
- 1 teaspoon pyrethrum dip (concentration on label should be about 1%)

Mix together and shampoo your dog as described on pages 54–56. Leave the shampoo on your dog for 10 minutes. Place him in his crate or, on a warm day, take him for a walk. Don't let him get chilled. After the 10 minutes, rinse thoroughly.

Grooming **57**

Skunk Smell Remover Shampoo

If your dog gets sprayed by a skunk, this shampoo will help get rid of the smell.

- 1 pint 3% household peroxide
- 4 tablespoons baking soda
- 1 tablespoon dishwashing liquid (grease-cutting type)

Mix together and shampoo your dog's coat. Leave the mixture on the coat for 10 minutes and rinse thoroughly. A second application may be needed in some cases. *Warning! It is not safe to store this mixture. Throw out any you don't use!*

The hair coats of some dogs become tangled or matted if not brushed frequently. If mud, burrs, twigs, pieces of dry grass, or other things get caught in the coat, the hair can snarl around them. Without regular grooming, mats and tangles have time to set. When a dog's coat becomes snarled, tangled, and matted, grooming is hard and time consuming for his owner, and very painful and unpleasant for him.

This section contains suggestions for grooming the different kinds of hair coats dogs can have. The suggestions are for house dogs that stay relatively clean. If your dog spends a lot of time outside, you should comb and brush him more often.

Brushing and Combing Equipment

Your dog's coat length and type will help you determine the brushing and combing tools you need:

Slicker brush. Slicker brushes have a handle and bent, fine wire bristles set in a cushioned base. They are used on light- to medium-coated dogs to remove dead hair, light tangles, and mats.

Brushing and combing remove dead, loose hair, stimulate the skin and hair follicles, and give you an opportunity to check for fleas and blemishes.

Bristle brush. Bristle brushes are made of nylon or a combination of nylon and brass bristles. One variety has a handle; another kind fits into your palm. The nylon type is used for general brushing and the combination type for deep cleaning.

Pin brush. Pin brushes have rubber-tipped wire bristles set in a cushioned base. They're excellent for thick and long coats.

Palm brush. Palm brushes are flexible and fit over your hand like a glove. They come with either sisal bristles or slicker bristles, or with sisal bristles on one side and wire bristles on the other.

Shampoo and massage gloves. Shampoo and massage gloves are used during bathing to distribute shampoo and cleanse deeply. On a dry coat, they stimulate the natural coat oils and blood circulation and help remove dead hair, tangles, and mats. The gloves work especially well for hard-to-reach areas and

Grooming Tools

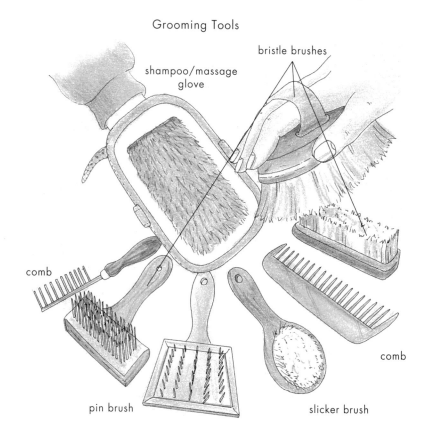

shampoo/massage glove

bristle brushes

comb

comb

pin brush

slicker brush

on bony areas such as the legs and face. Their bristles or nubs are made of a rigid rubber or plastic.

Comb. Regular combs are made for coats of varying thicknesses and lengths. Depending on the space between the teeth, a comb is described as coarse, medium, fine, or flea. Some combs are divided in the middle, with half coarse and half medium, or half medium and half fine. Flea combs remove fleas from an already groomed coat. Thick or rough coats require combs with the teeth farther apart. Short-haired breeds require combs with the teeth closer together. Combs are made of metal; some are coated with Teflon. There are full-length combs and combs with handles.

Care of Different Coat Types

Here are some tips for brushing and combing. If your dog is a mixed breed, use the tools and techniques that suit his coat type.

Short or Smooth Coat

All short-coated dogs, such as Dobermans, Beagles, and Dalmatians, should be brushed at least once a week. First, comb the hair two or three times in the direction it grows with a fine-toothed comb. Next, brush the dog several times, in both directions, with a bristle brush. Wipe him down with a slightly damp towel. You may also spray him lightly with coat conditioner. Wipe him again with a clean, dry towel. Use caution not to spray near his face. Instead, wipe this area with a towel that has a little conditioner on it.

Smooth-coated breeds can also be brushed with a grooming glove. Dogs enjoy vigorous brushing with this glove.

Brush the complete dog several times in the direction of hair growth. Wipe him down with a slightly damp towel. As a final step, spray a very small amount of coat conditioner on a clean, slightly damp towel and rub over the coat, in the direction that the

Be Careful!

A grooming glove with wire bristles may scratch the skin of a very smooth-coated dog such as a Doberman Pinscher.

hair grows. Turn the towel over and wipe him down several more times to be sure no oily residue remains that can stain your furniture, carpet, or clothing.

Wire-Haired or Rough-Haired Coat

Wire-haired or rough-haired dogs should be groomed once a week with a slicker brush. This includes Bouviers and most terriers. First, brush the complete dog in the direction that the hair grows, and then in the opposite direction. Repeat this several times and you'll loosen the dead hair, dirt, and debris.

Long, Dense Coat

Dogs with long, dense coats that stand out from the body should be combed and brushed twice a week. Poodles, Bichons, and Chow Chows are among the breeds in this group. Comb with a coarse comb and then brush with a pin brush.

Long, Silky Coat

Dogs with long, silky coats that tangle easily, such as the Maltese, Shih Tzu, Lhasa Apso, and Afghan, should be brushed every day. Fine-toothed combs and pin brushes work well. If the coat begins to tangle, apply tangle remover and gently try to comb through it again.

© ISABELLE FRANCAIS

Corded Coat

A corded coat is one that falls naturally into separate cords, like a string mop. These dogs are never combed out; instead, they're washed and conditioned with their cords intact. Breeds with this type of coat are the Poodle, Puli, and Komondor.

Trimming or Clipping the Coat

Medium- to long-coated purebred dogs are usually trimmed into the typical pattern for that breed. If

Trying a traditional clip on a mixed breed can be fun.

Ear leather. The skin of a dog's ear.

Ear Cleaner

- ½ cup isopropyl alcohol
- ½ cup water
- 1½ teaspoons boric acid — powdered blue food coloring

Mix ingredients together in a bottle. Be sure the boric acid is completely dissolved. Dip a toothpick into a small bottle of food coloring. Put the toothpick into the bottle, cover it, and shake. Remove the toothpick and throw it in the trash. This will add enough color so that you'll be able to tell the ear cleaner from water. Pour the mixture into another bottle with a small top and mark the outside "Dog Ear Cleaner. Contains Isopropyl Alcohol. Not for Internal Use." Keep this and any dog-grooming products out of the reach of small children, who might find them tempting to eat or drink.

you have a mixed-breed dog with a coat that will take trimming nicely, you can have a lot of fun with it. One time you can have a Schnauzer cut, the next time a Poodle cut, the next time one of the terrier cuts.

Trimming the coat of a dog is complicated and requires skill and practice. I suggest taking the dog to a groomer for his haircuts. If you don't have the money in your budget for a groomer's charges, ask the groomer if there are any chores you can do to pay for the cut. Maybe you can trade your services for his or hers by washing and drying dogs, or sweeping up the shop. Also ask if you could watch or help. It's always fun to learn new things.

Ear Care

Check your dog's ears regularly. Does the *ear leather* look and feel healthy, or is it thickened, crusted, or showing signs of a rash? Look down in the opening of the ear. You should see only a clear, light, waxlike substance. If the ear is reddened or has an unpleasant odor or any secretions that aren't normal, your veterinarian should check for mites or infection.

Don't put anything into the dog's ear channel to clean it, unless instructed by your veterinarian. However, you can use cotton balls soaked with ear cleaner around the opening and on the ear leather. You may never have problems with your dog's ears if you keep them clean and have them checked regularly by the veterinarian.

Toenail Care

Dogs that wear down their toenails by walking on concrete or other rough surfaces need to have their toenails trimmed less often than dogs that hardly ever get off the carpet. Problems can develop in the dog's foot if his nails are overgrown. As a general rule, trimming once a month is sufficient.

Toenail Clipping Equipment

Before you begin, assemble toenail clippers, styptic powder, leash, and collar. Ask an experienced adult to help you choose the type of clipper that's best for your dog's nail size.

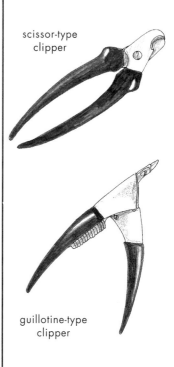

scissor-type clipper

guillotine-type clipper

Clipping Your Dog's Toenails

Before you try to clip your dog's toenails, have an experienced adult show you how. The first few times you do the clipping yourself, have an adult help you.

Ask your helper to hold the dog by his collar, with the leash attached.

If your dog's nails are a light color, you should be able to see a pink area through the nail. This is called the quick. Clip the portion of the nail just *outside* of this pink area. If your dog's nails are black, first cut off the hooked portion and then gradually clip a tiny bit at

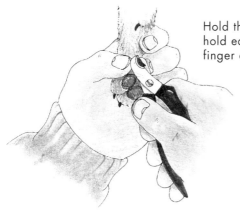

Hold the dog's paw in your hand, then hold each toe between your thumb and finger as you clip the nail tip.

Ask an adult to help you when you trim your dog's nails. If you're not sure where the quick is, trim only the tip of the nail and repeat in one week.

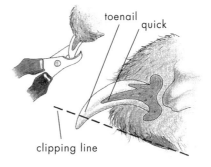

toenail

quick

clipping line

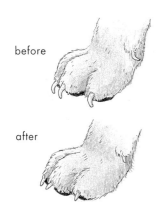
before

after

Trim nails so that they just clear the floor when your dog is standing on all four feet.

Reassure and Praise

Reassure your dog and praise him when he remains calm. Praise him every time you clip a nail and he doesn't resist.

a time. If you just slightly cut the quick, the nail will bleed a bit, and the dog may flinch. Reassure him and use the styptic powder to stop the bleeding. A light nick in the quick is easily forgotten.

Don't forget to trim the *dewclaw* nail on the inside of each front foot. Some dogs also have one or two extra dewclaws on the inside of each hind foot.

You can tell when you've trimmed your dog's nails to the right length by standing him on a hard surface. If each nail just clears the surface, they're the proper length.

Tooth Care

You should check and clean your dog's teeth regularly. Cleaning two times a week will help maintain healthy teeth.

Puppies begin life with no teeth. At three weeks they begin to get their first set of 28 teeth. These small teeth start to be replaced when the pup is about four months old. By six months, most breeds have 42 new teeth. When the puppy is teething, he has the irresistible urge to chew everything in sight.

Check the pup's teeth during this time to be sure he's not keeping his baby teeth along with his adult teeth. If he is, this may have to be corrected by the veterinarian.

Checking Your Dog's Teeth

Teach your puppy at an early age to accept the routine opening of his mouth. First, tell him "teeth," and lift just his lips for a few seconds. If the pup remains quiet, open his mouth and run your fingers across his teeth for a few seconds. The best way to do this is to put one hand over his muzzle, with your thumb just behind his canine tooth. With the other hand, hold his bottom jaw so that your thumbs are touching. Say "teeth," push in slightly with your thumbs, and raise his upper jaw.

Spend only a minute with your dog's mouth open. Praise him if he doesn't resist. Repeat this over the next week until your puppy will allow you to examine all of his teeth.

Cleaning Your Dog's Teeth

Introduce your dog to the toothbrush gently. Say "teeth," open his mouth, touch the toothbrush to a few of his teeth, and brush lightly. You may also use a rough washcloth wrapped around your index finger in place of the brush. If the dog remains calm, praise him while you're working in his mouth. Gradually add toothpaste or baking soda to the brush and gently clean the teeth. Don't forget to praise the dog if he isn't resisting you.

If at any time your dog develops a buildup of tartar, or his gums become red or are bleeding, check with your veterinarian as soon as possible. If caught early, a routine cleaning by your veterinarian could halt serious gum disease.

Checking the Anal Glands

If you have ever smelled the perfume a skunk leaves behind, it might surprise you to learn that your dog also has scent glands, which leave his very own special scent. One anal gland is located on either side of the lower half of the *anus*. These glands contain a substance that's released when your dog defecates. This strong-smelling *secretion* is the signature of your dog to other dogs that pass by.

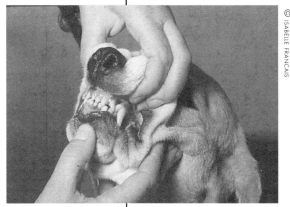

© ISABELLE FRANCAIS

Teach your puppy to let you handle his mouth.

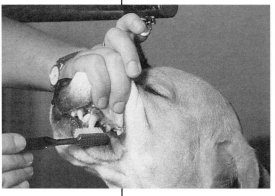

© ISABELLE FRANCAIS

Cleaning your dog's teeth is an important part of his health care.

The anal glands can become *impacted* and cause discomfort to your dog. When this happens, he may scoot his rear across the floor or lick the area under his tail to relieve the discomfort. If you have a dog that has this problem frequently, ask your veterinarian to teach you the correct way to *express* these anal sacs. It's a simple procedure, but since every dog is a little bit different, your veterinarian can show you the proper method for your dog. You might want a clothespin for your nose, but you will have a grateful dog when you are through.

Your Dog's Good Health

CHAPTER

It's a good idea to take your puppy to your veterinarian as soon as possible after you receive him. Your veterinarian can perform a thorough exam to determine his general state of health, as well as to give "preventive maintenance" — de-worming and immunizations.

Your Puppy's First Visit to the Veterinarian

Your veterinarian will need the following information for this visit, all of which should have been given to you by the person who sold you the puppy.

- When and from whom did you get the puppy?

- What is his breed and age?

- What has he been eating?

- What vaccinations has he received so far?

Preventing Health Problems

Take the time to check your dog every day, looking for any changes from his normal appearance or behavior. If you see any of the changes described in the next section, ask your veterinarian what to do. The veterinarian is trained to diagnose illnesses and injuries and prescribe the proper treatment. If the information you provide is accurate and detailed, the veterinarian has a better chance of pinpointing the problem. Any little detail could be just what your veterinarian needs to identify your dog's difficulty. In an emergency situation, however, call for help immediately.

Signs of Illness

Learn to recognize the signs that tell you your dog may be sick.

Change in Eating Habits

Have your dog's eating habits changed? Occasionally a healthy dog will turn down his normal meal. If your dog refuses his regular diet more than once, though, it may be cause for your concern. Loss of appetite could

Watch your puppy or dog for signs of discomfort. He may be sick and need treatment from your veterinarian.

be a sign of bacterial or viral infection; a general fever; a blockage of the digestive tract; or a problem with the mouth, teeth, or gums in the form of an infection, an injury, or penetration of a foreign object.

Abnormal Urination or Bowel Movements

Are your dog's urination or bowel movements different than normal: more frequent, less frequent, different color, different consistency, performed only with difficulty? A urinary problem could be caused by an infection or abnormality in the liver, kidney, or urinary/reproductive tract. Abnormal bowel movements such as diarrhea, constipation, and changes in frequency or color can be caused by many things, including intestinal parasites, infections, certain infectious diseases, stress, and change of diet.

Vomiting

Is your dog vomiting food, stomach fluids, or blood? This could be caused by eating something poisonous, spoiled food, intestinal parasites, infections, inflammation of the intestinal tract, or disease of the kidney or liver.

Change in Behavior

Is your dog acting frightened or irritable? Is your normally playful dog acting depressed and lethargic? Is he trembling, anxious, stumbling? In all of these cases, he might be in pain from disease or injury.

Panting, Breathing Problems

Is your dog panting excessively, having problems breathing normally, or coughing? This may be caused by heartworm infection, pain, heart disease, respiratory disease, stress, or obesity, among other things. If your dog has been involved in hard play or running, it's natural for him to pant until he cools down. If he continues to pant, or if his breathing becomes very shallow, he could have heat prostration and need emergency care. Also, females about to give birth pant heavily as they go into labor.

Calling Your Veterinarian

Your veterinarian is trained to listen to the symptoms you have noticed and perform a thorough examination to diagnose your dog's problem. If your dog has any of the above symptoms, call and ask your veterinarian or advice.

When you call your veterinarian you may be asked what the dog's temperature is and if he is dehydrated. If you have this information when you call, it will assist the veterinarian. But if your dog is in undue stress, don't waste time — get him to the veterinarian immediately.

Taking Your Dog's Temperature

Take your dog's temperature with a lubricated rectal thermometer. If it's a glass thermometer you must shake it down until the temperature is below 98°F. If it's a battery-operated digital thermometer you usually just have to push the button twice to clear the previous temperature reading.

Hold your dog's tail with one hand and gently insert the lubricated thermometer into his rectum to a depth of 1 inch. Be sure to hold onto the thermometer. Your dog should be lying down if possible. If he's standing, he might sit down and you could lose control of the thermometer. If your dog is fidgety, ask someone to help you by holding him.

Watch for Signs of Illness

If you notice any discharge, swelling, redness, unusual odor, sneezing, coughing, hair loss, dripping saliva or urine, or anything else that isn't normal for your dog, be sure to contact your veterinarian at once.

A digital thermometer will usually "beep" when it has reached a constant temperature. A glass thermometer should be left in place for about one minute. A dog's normal temperature is 101.5°F; it can vary slightly, however, between 100 and 102°. If your dog has been very active or is excited, his temperature will be slightly elevated. In this case you won't get a true reading until he has calmed or cooled down.

Checking for Dehydration

To check for dehydration, lift your dog's skin over his shoulder blades and let it drop back in place by itself. If it falls back quickly, the dog is probably not dehydrated. If it falls back slowly or stays in a small pile, the dog could be dehydrated. Check your dog's mouth to see if his gums are dry or sticky, which also indicates dehydration. It's critical that a dehydrated dog receive veterinary help immediately to prevent him from going into *shock*.

Learning to Stand for the Veterinarian's Exam

A squirming, wiggling, unmanageable puppy is hard for the veterinarian to examine.

You can easily teach your puppy to stand for an examination on the veterinarian's table while you're holding him. The training is done at home. First, put a soft buckle collar on the puppy and let him walk around for a short time. Don't leave him alone while he's getting used to the collar. Don't attach a leash yet.

Gently insert the lubricated thermometer into the rectum to a depth of about an inch.

Warning!

You can injure your dog if you don't know how to take his temperature properly. Always get a knowledgeable adult to help you.

When your puppy has become familiar with the collar, prepare a raised platform that's just 18 to 24 inches from the floor. The distance must not be over 24 inches to start. An airline dog crate works well. Place a rubber doormat or a piece of scrap carpet on the top so that the puppy will have good footing. If necessary, tape the mat or carpet to the crate so that it doesn't slide or slip.

You should be in a carpeted room or outside on the grass; that way, if the puppy falls or jumps, he has little chance of being hurt. Clip a lightweight leash to his collar as a safety precaution.

Gently pick up the puppy with your right hand under his neck, your finger and thumb also holding his collar. Support the puppy under his tummy with your

Teach your puppy to stand for examination. Practice on a surface that's not slippery and that won't scare him.

left hand. The puppy must feel secure. Place him on the mat. Keep both hands in the same position to prevent him from jumping or falling off. Praise immediately if he remains calm by saying something in a happy voice — maybe, "*Good* dog." Don't worry if your puppy wants to lie down or sit, as long as he remains calm.

If the puppy is rambunctious or is afraid, scold him with a firm "no" and place him firmly exactly where you want him to be. Don't be rough; your voice and actions must be *firm* but not rough. Don't try to comfort him by saying, "It's okay." This will only reinforce the disorderly behavior or fear. Scratch the puppy under his tummy with your left hand and under his neck with your right hand. Keep this position only for a minute.

Remove the puppy from the "table" and cuddle him. In a few minutes, repeat the whole procedure, placing the puppy on the table again. Remember *to praise immediately whenever the puppy is calm.* Scratching the puppy helps soothe him.

If the puppy has been remaining calm, start to place him in a standing position. At all times, keep your hands in the same position. Gradually increase the time to about three minutes. Even the most unruly puppy can usually be trained in one lesson.

Immunizations

We can boost the immune system of puppies and dogs to provide greater protection against many diseases. This is done by taking them to the veterinarian to get the proper vaccinations when they're young, and then to get booster doses periodically throughout their lives. A vaccination is an injection (a "shot") that can help the puppy or dog fight off certain diseases. Many canine diseases are highly contagious and can be transmitted between dogs by contact with an infected animal, with his urine or feces, or with something he

Helpful Hint for Veterinarian Visits

Veterinarians' examination tables are often made of stainless steel or Formica. These surfaces are slippery, cold, and even terrifying to some puppies. Why not take along a small doormat your puppy is familiar with when you make your first few visits to the veterinarian? The familiar surface will help ease your puppy's fears.

has recently touched. Some diseases are transmitted through the air when a dog coughs or sneezes.

A puppy is protected against certain diseases while he is still nursing his mother. The mother passes on some disease resistance through her milk. Sometimes this protection lasts a few weeks after weaning, but not always. It depends on how high the mother's defenses against the diseases are. Your puppy's vaccination schedule must be planned according to his age and when he was weaned.

There's a higher incidence of some diseases in certain regions. Sometimes there are even epidemics. Your veterinarian is aware of the diseases that are prevalent in your area and can advise you about when the puppy or dog will need his first vaccinations and subsequent boosters.

Many of the diseases described here are fatal to dogs. Most of these or similar diseases can also be found in other animals such as the cat, fox, coyote, wolf, ferret, mink, weasel, skunk, badger, otter, and raccoon. It's never wise to let your dog come into

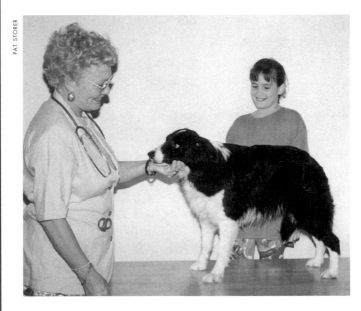

Your veterinarian will appreciate your work to train your dog to stand still for examination.

contact with a wild animal, because the wild animal has not been vaccinated. Here are some of the diseases for which you can vaccinate your puppy or dog.

Distemper (D)

All dogs must be vaccinated against distemper. This disease is found all over the world, and often affects puppies that haven't been vaccinated. It's almost always fatal. This virus affects the respiratory, nervous, and gastrointestinal systems. It's highly *contagious;* it's spread by an airborne virus as well as in bodily secretions and feces.

Contagious. *Capable of being spread from one dog to another.*

Canine Infectious Hepatitis (H)

This disease is found in dogs and related wild animals. It can be transmitted if a dog's mouth or nose comes into contact with a sick animal's body secretions, or with external parasites that have infected the sick dog. It's difficult to disinfect against this virus. A dog that does recover from it can still pass the virus to other dogs for up to nine months.

Adenovirus (A-1)

This disease can cause severe damage to the liver and blood vessels. It's highly contagious and very painful for the puppy or dog. It's often found in combination with parainfluenza and bordatella.

Parainfluenza (P) or Tracheobronchitis

This highly contagious disease of the respiratory tract is often called kennel cough, although the most common kennel cough is a combination of several viruses. It's spread directly between dogs through airborne viruses from coughing and sneezing, or indirectly from anything that has been in contact with the viruses, such as dishes, people, food, and water bowls. The dog develops a dry, hacking cough caused by excessive mucus. The infection can be mild or very severe. Mild forms may disappear in one to two weeks. More severe cases can require hospitalization and can develop into more serious problems, such as pneumonia.

Bordatella

Bordatella is most often found in combination with other viruses, such as parainfluenza and adenovirus. It causes severe hacking coughs. See "Adenovirus," on page 75.

Leptospirosis (L)

This highly contagious disease can cause damage to the liver, kidneys, and gastrointestinal system. It's spread by mucus, saliva, and urine, as well as by contact with bedding, dishes, or anything that an infected dog has touched. Wild animals, including rodents, can also be carriers of this disease.

Parvovirus (PV)

This very contagious disease is known for often causing death in puppies. It often begins suddenly, without warning. Adult dogs can harbor the virus and show few symptoms but still pass on the disease to other dogs and puppies via their feces. Dogs that survive after proper medical treatment can continue to spread the virus for some time. The virus can also stay alive for several months on surfaces touched by the dog. There are special disinfectants that are used to treat areas exposed to parvovirus.

Coronavirus (CV)

This contagious disease affects the gastrointestinal system, causing high fever, dehydration, and vomiting. With proper medical care a dog can survive this disease, but he can infect other animals for several months afterward through his feces.

Lyme Disease

Lyme disease is caused by an organism carried inside certain species of ticks that are most often found in wooded and grassy areas. Ticks live on the blood of other animals. The organism that causes Lyme disease spends part of its life cycle inside wild birds and rodents. A tick that has dined on the blood of an infected bird or mouse will transmit the organism to other animals, including dogs and people. Dogs that are infected can be treated with antibiotics, but often the treatment must be continued for a very long time.

Rabies

This virus can occur in dogs, cats, and other mammals. It is transmissible to humans. It spreads through contact with an infected animal's saliva.

Most states have laws requiring all dogs to be vaccinated against this deadly disease. There's no treatment for rabies in animals. Wild animals can transmit the disease to domestic pets and livestock.

Planning Your Puppy's Immunization Program

When you buy your puppy or dog, you should receive a record of all of the vaccinations he has received to date. A few breeds are very susceptible to one or more of the diseases listed above. If you're purchasing a less common breed, the person selling you the dog should know, by experience, if that breed has a higher degree of sensitivity to a particular disease. Your veterinarian might not be aware of this greater sensitivity. Take the schedule of vaccines the puppy or dog has been given so far to your veterinarian soon after you bring the dog home. Tell the veterinarian about anything unusual you have learned about your breed's special health needs. The

Warning!

Be sure never to handle a wild animal. Sick wild animals often appear friendly and gentle, but they act this way because of their sickness. Touching them or even coming close to them can cause them to bite you. If they have rabies, you will probably be infected and will need medical help immediately.

veterinarian will review this information and plan a comprehensive schedule for vaccinating your new pet.

A vaccine can be for protection from a single disease or a combination of several diseases. Your veterinarian may have a preference for single or combination vaccines. The incidence of diseases in your area will indicate for which your dog will need to be vaccinated. The age of your dog, his breed, his vaccination record, and the prevalence of diseases in your area will determine how often, and in what sequence, he should be vaccinated. Puppies can receive their first dose against some of the diseases as early as five weeks. Often one to four more doses will be needed every two to four weeks. Boosters are then given annually or semiannually according to your dog's risk. Your veterinarian will also suggest a time for the dog's rabies vaccine or booster. In some states with a high incidence of rabies, this is given as early as 12 weeks of age; most often it's done between four and six months.

The chart below is a sample immunization schedule for puppies and dogs. Remember that your veterinarian is the person to choose the proper schedule for your pet.

Health Tip

Dogs that frequently come into contact with other dogs — perhaps at trials, shows, or boarding kennels — or that live in an area where an outbreak occurs may need a booster (except for rabies) every six months in place of the annual booster.

Age	Vaccinate Against
5 weeks	Parvovirus
6, 8, 10, 12 weeks	Distemper, hepatitis, adenovirus cough, parainfluenza, parvovirus
14, 16, 18 weeks	Distemper, hepatitis, leptospirosis, adenovirus cough, parainfluenza, parvovirus
3–6 months	Rabies
Yearly booster	Distemper, hepatitis, leptospirosis, adenovirus cough, parainfluenza, parvovirus, rabies

This is one example of an immunization schedule. Your veterinarian may have a different schedule for your dog.

Parasite Control — Internal and External

Your dog is irresistibly delicious to a group of creepy creatures. Fleas, ticks, mites, flies, and worms outside and inside your dog live on his blood and tissues. Some of these can make your dog very sick, or even kill him. Some of them are transmissible to humans, and that means you! While you're at your veterinarian's office, your dog will probably be checked for parasites. Your veterinarian can recommend a safe treatment program for your pet.

External Parasites

Fleas, ticks, mites, and flies are the most commonly found parasites on puppies and dogs. There are so many different treatments on the market today that it's difficult to figure out which ones will work on which pests. There are dips, powders, sprays, salves, shampoos, collars, oral pills, and topical applications.

The length of effectiveness of a treatment depends on the prevention method and, in some cases, the exposure of the dog to wet weather.

If you live in an area where fleas are a serious problem, your veterinarian will be able to advise you on which product will be best for your dog. This is important because young puppies can be sensitive to the chemicals found in certain products. Your veterinarian might suggest routine bathing with a flea shampoo followed by a spray or dip; an oral pill that's given two or three times a week; a small topical application between the dog's shoulders every month; or one of the other products.

If ticks, mites, and flies are a concern, you will be steered toward products that will help clear up the infestation. Some of the products can only be obtained from a veterinarian, because they're prescription items.

Pyrethrum-based products are among the safest compounds to use. They're made from a particular chrysanthemum flower. They are fast acting but have little staying power. Sometimes they're mixed with other chemicals to increase the length of their effectiveness.

Other chemicals can be longer lasting but have risks as well. Discuss their safety and lasting qualities with your veterinarian.

Natural Alternatives for Flea Control

Here are some natural methods for controlling fleas in and around your house and on your dog.

Outside Your House

Diatomaceous earth is a low-cost product that can be used outside for flea control. Talk to your parents about trying this method in your yard. Diatomaceous earth is a very fine white powdery substance available in 25-pound bags from stores that carry pool supplies. It coats the fleas and cuts them with the sharp edges of its particles. The fleas soon die.

Diatomaceous earth is applied to the yard using a broadcast spreader. Do not breathe in the dust, because diatomaceous earth is *harmful to your lungs*. Wear a face mask to be safe. Do this once a week for three weeks, then repeat every three months during warm weather, every six months during cool weather. If it rains, you'll have to repeat the application.

Inside Your House

Boric acid kills fleas and their *larvae*. It's found in borax, which you can buy at most grocery stores in the laundry detergent section. Put it in a shaker can and

Larva. *The stage of some insects' lives when they have just hatched and look like worms.*

sprinkle on carpets, furniture, and mattresses. Don't forget to sprinkle it under pillows, cushions, and furniture. Leave it on for a day, then vacuum it up. Repeat every two or three weeks for two months, then once every three months during the summer, once every six months during cooler weather.

Herbal Crate Pad

An herbal crate pad might help keep fleas out of your dog's crate.

> 2 parts pennyroyal leaves
> 1 part wormwood leaves
> 1 part rosemary leaves
> 1 part thyme leaves
> 50 parts pine shavings (not sawdust)

Measure the bottom of your dog's crate. Add 6 inches to the measurement of each side. If your crate measures 20 by 27, for example, your final measurement will be 26 by 33. Choose a fabric that's durable, such as denim or canvas. You need enough for four pieces. Most of this fabric comes in widths of 45 to 60 inches.

Cut four pieces of the size you need. Put two aside. Put the right sides (the "outsides") of other two pieces of material together. Sew around the edges, leaving an opening of about 6 inches on one side. Mix the herbs with the pine shavings and fill the pad to about 3 inches thick. Sew up the opening. Make a cover for this pad following the above sewing directions, using the two reserved pieces of fabric. Turn the cover inside out and press it flat with your hands. Cut two strips of Velcro exactly the length of the opening. Center one strip on the inside of the opening on one side of the cover. Sew in place. Repeat with the other piece of Velcro. Fold

Laundry

Wash the outer cover when needed. Never let it get too dirty, or the dirt may seep through into the pillow itself.

the stuffed pillow in half, insert it through the opening, and flatten it out. Press the open end of the cover together so that the Velcro pieces connect, and place the pillow in the dog's crate.

Internal Parasites

Puppies and dogs can get various kinds of parasites that live inside their bodies. We hear about de-worming so often that we might underestimate how important it is to a dog's good health. Most types of internal parasites are "worms" of several different types. Some species live part of their lives in the dog's gastrointestinal tract, and some live in his heart. Some species can migrate through his body and do damage to vital organs and tissues. These creatures eat the bodily fluids and tissues of your dog.

You should keep your dog free of parasites for his health and yours. Many of the parasites spend one or more stages of their lives in the bodies of other living creatures, such as mice, fleas, mosquitoes, rabbits, and other dogs. Some develop in moist conditions in grass, dirt, or concrete. When the parasites reach maturity inside your dog, some reproduce and pass eggs or larvae out of the body in his feces, while others circulate in his bloodstream.

To keep your puppy or dog on the best parasite control program, visit your veterinarian regularly. Dogs that don't come into contact with other dogs, or with the places that other dogs have visited, need a parasite checkup at least twice a year. Some veterinarians will ask you to bring in a fresh stool sample for a microscopic examination. This exam will show what intestinal parasites, if any, your dog has in his body. If he needs to be treated, your veterinarian will know the proper medication for those specific worms.

Skin and Hair Disorders

Skin diseases make your dog uncomfortable because his skin is dry and itchy or inflamed. He scratches and bites at the affected part, sometimes until that area is raw and bleeding. Here are some of the most common skin conditions.

Ringworm

Ringworm isn't a worm at all. It's a fungus that causes hair loss and skin irritation. The dog's skin can become dry and scaly, or in some cases inflamed and moist. Often, the ringworm is in a dry, circular, hairless patch. Other times, the dog can lose much of the hair on his entire body. The ringworm can even get between his toes, around his eyes, or in his ears and cause severe discomfort.

Ringworm disease is highly contagious to people and other animals, especially cats. There is no preventive for this disease, but your veterinarian can treat it with baths, applications to the affected areas, and oral medication. Your dog's bedding will also have to be treated.

Flea Allergy Dermatitis

Some dogs are extremely sensitive to flea saliva. Bites from a few fleas can be so irritating to a dog that he chews himself constantly. The areas of the dog most commonly affected first are at the *croup,* the base of the tail, and the thighs. Some dogs roll, rub, scratch, and chew until they cause severe damage to their skin and underlying tissues. These areas can then become infected with bacteria and get rapidly worse.

You can prevent flea allergy dermatitis by keeping your dog and his environment free of fleas. A dog with

Heartworm Cycle

The heartworm lives in the dog's heart. If you could see a cross-section of a dog infected with heartworms, the worms would look like 5-inch white spaghetti. The female heartworms pass an immature larval form that circulates in the dog's bloodstream. When a mosquito bites the dog, the blood it takes in contains these larvae, which further develop in the mosquito and then enter the bloodstream of the mosquito's next victim.

the disease can be treated by the veterinarian, and his home environment must be also treated with flea control products that contain a growth hormone regulator. Your veterinarian will tell which products to use.

Pyroderma

Pyroderma is an infection of the skin caused by certain bacteria. Some breeds have skin folds that create a warm, moist home for bacteria. A hot spot is a moist sore on the dog's body that may have begun when he received a scratch or cut. Both of these conditions should be treated by your veterinarian, who can clean and disinfect the area and prescribe the proper medication. If your dog has chronic skin infections in skin folds, your veterinarian may recommend surgery.

Mange

Sarcoptic mange is caused by a microscopic mite that burrows into the dog's skin and lays its eggs. It's also called scabies. Sarcoptic mange causes crusty patches on a dog's body. This mite is very contagious and can be transferred to other dogs and humans who come into contact with the dog, his housing, and his grooming tools. Your veterinarian can look at a small scraping from the dog's skin under a microscope and determine if he has sarcoptic mange. It's treated with special shampoos and medicines prescribed by your veterinarian. The area in which the dog has lived must be also treated with a parasiticide that kills the mites.

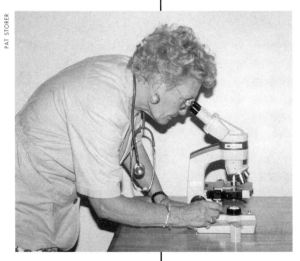

Your veterinarian can diagnose skin problems by looking at samples under a microscope.

Demodectic mange is caused by a microscopic mite that's naturally found on all dogs in small numbers. These mites rarely harm the dog if he is healthy. If his resistance is low because he isn't healthy, however, the number of mites grows, causing hair loss in affected areas, such as the head and feet. Sometimes this will correct itself in a month or two, but it's best to have your veterinarian look at the dog. The veterinarian can take a small skin scraping, look at it under the microscope, and prescribe the proper treatment.

Preventing Accidents

The entire area to which your puppy or dog has access must be made safe. This means you must check for anything that could be harmful to him, and make sure that all exits are kept closed.

Try to be aware of what your dog is doing at all times. He must not be able to open a cupboard or reach any item that could be poisonous such as drain cleaners, soaps, detergents, bleaches, chemicals of any type, medicines, and more. Keep doors closed to areas that contain hazardous materials such as antifreeze, fuel, paint, fertilizer, weed or insect killers, or small items such as nuts, bolts, nails, broken glass, and plastic bags. Fences and gates should be checked to be sure there is absolutely no way the dog can dig, squeeze, jump, or climb out.

Here are some other tips for keeping your puppy or a dog safe:

- Electrical cords of all types should be out of reach or enclosed in PVC pipe or conduit.

- Don't let your dog have toys with small parts or toys that can be chewed and swallowed.

- Make sure your dog's collar can't get caught on bucket handles, fence wires, dishes hooked in the door of his crate, or any other place.

Special Care for Puppies

- Regular checkups to be sure he is growing properly

- A safe environment, free of harmful objects and substances

- Special nutrition for healthy growth, and a diet without too many treats that will spoil his appetite

- Opportunities to be socialized with other people and dogs from a very early age

- Never leave your dog alone when he's tied or chained.

- If you can't be sure that your puppy is safe, place him in his crate or pen.

Tattooing and Microchipping

If you purchase a puppy that's registered with the American Kennel Club, he should have some sort of permanent identification. The most common type of identification is a code consisting of numbers and maybe some letters that are tattooed on the dog. The code itself is designated by the breeder or owner and identifies an individual puppy. The tattoo is usually placed on the bare skin on the inside of the thigh, or on the abdomen. Dogs that have drop ears are often tattooed on the inside of the ear leather.

Microchips are a new addition to the system of dog identification. A microchip is a tiny glass capsule about the size of a grain and a half of rice. Inside the capsule is a miniature copper antenna, a *capacitor,* and a tiny microchip that contains a special identification number. Only one microchip is made with that number in the world. A veterinarian uses a special syringe to

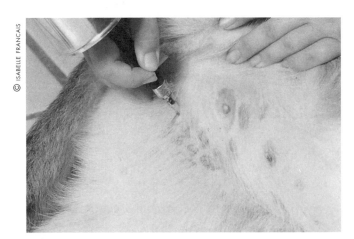

© ISABELLE FRANCAIS

A tattoo permanently identifies your dog.

insert the microchip under the skin above the dog's shoulder blades. When a *scanner* is passed over the dog, it reads and reports the ID number on its screen.

If you lose your dog and someone finds him, the tattoo or microchip number is your means of identifying him. Microchips and tattoos can be registered with certain agencies that notify the owner when a dog with an ID number is reported found.

Should You Breed Your Dog?

You must make a very important decision when you add a puppy or dog to your family. Will your dog be allowed to breed someday? Unless you become a professional breeder, your answer should be "no."

Bad Reasons for Allowing Your Dog to Breed

Many of the reasons people give for allowing their dogs to breed are simply not true. The following reasons are all *false.*

1. *A female dog will be healthier and happier if she's allowed to have at least one litter before she's spayed.* There is absolutely no foundation to this statement. Breeding won't make your dog a better pet, but spaying her might. In addition, dogs spayed after the first heat are more likely to develop mammary tumors than those spayed prior to the first heat.

2. *It's cruel to neuter a male dog.* Not true. In fact, you might not like some of his natural behaviors if he isn't neutered or if he's ever used for breeding.

3. *Our dog should have puppies because I want my children to see the miracle of birth.* Children can see the miracle of birth on TV on one of the nature channels.

Special Care for Older Dogs

- A very low-fat diet (unless he's very active) to prevent obesity

- For an overweight dog, a diet and exercise program designed by your veterinarian to help him lose weight without harming his health

- Frequent checkups by your veterinarian

The Arithmetic of Breeding

If all 25 million baby pets are born in equal numbers of males and females, and if every female puppy or kitten born within the past year begins breeding when she's old enough, and if she has three babies each time, there would be enough puppies and kittens to be laid end to end around the world more than one and one-half times less than 18 months from today.

Puberty. *The age at which an animal becomes able to breed.*

Overpopulation, Homelessness, Death

It's getting harder and harder to find homes for puppies. The classified sections in newspapers are filled with ads offering puppies and dogs.

The Humane Society reports that over 70,000 puppies and kittens are born *every day* in the United States alone because people didn't prevent their pets from mating. This is an astounding 25 million puppies and kittens a year.

No wonder animal shelters are filled to capacity. No wonder so many puppies are euthanized each year because shelters can't find homes for them. And — these figures don't include stray or abandoned animals, which will mate if they aren't neutered.

Spaying and Neutering

The sad statistics above should encourage you to have your dog neutered or spayed before he or she is capable of reproducing. You can have your dog spayed or neutered by your veterinarian or at a spay-neuter clinic. Some animal shelters provide inexpensive spay-neuter services; some are free or for a donation.

Dogs come into *puberty* between 6 and 12 months of age. At this time, they are capable of mating and producing puppies. Smaller breeds mature earlier than larger breeds, and dogs that run free usually mature earlier than those kept in confinement.

A puppy can be neutered or spayed as soon as the veterinarian feels that he or she will be safe under anesthesia. This could be as early as eight weeks of age. Dogs older than this can be neutered or spayed almost anytime if they're in good health, except when a female is in her estrus cycle or already pregnant.

Neutering Males

To neuter a male, the veterinarian surgically removes both of the *testicles*. If they have both descended into the *scrotum* it will be a relatively simple procedure. If one or both testicles haven't descended, the surgery is more complicated, and will be more costly.

Spaying Females

To spay a female, the veterinarian makes an abdominal *incision* and removes the reproductive tract, including the *ovaries* and *uterus*. This is a routine procedure for veterinarians.

Spay surgery on an overweight dog is more difficult for the veterinarian, and harder on the dog as well. If a female dog is close to coming into her estrus cycle, or is in her cycle, surgery can also be difficult. Your veterinarian may advise you to wait a few more weeks.

If you have your dog spayed *before* she has her first cycle, her nipples and vulva will remain juvenile in size and give a neat look to her tummy. If she cycles before the surgery, they'll be larger.

Care of a Pregnant Female and Her Puppies

If for some reason you end up with a pregnant dog, you'll need some basic information about caring for her and her puppies.

Getting Ready for the Birth

Birth takes place between 58 and 63 days after mating. The mother-to-be will need a comfortable area for *whelping*. Large dogs may need a specially constructed whelping box to prevent the mother from smashing a

Be Alert!

If your female dog comes into heat before you have her spayed, it's very important to keep her away from all unneutered males.

Special Care

Before you take your dog in for spaying or neutering, the veterinarian will give you important instructions about withholding your dog's food and water before the surgery. You will also get specific care instructions for when you take your dog home. Stitches are usually removed 10 to 14 days after surgery.

Whelp. *To give birth to puppies.*

baby if one gets trapped between her and the wall when she's lying down.

Labor and Birth

Dogs seem to give birth during the quietest time of day, when they're resting, often in the middle of the night. If there are no problems, the mother should be able to deliver and clean the puppies by herself.

If the female doesn't produce a puppy after she has been in labor for a couple of hours, or if she has been straining for more than an hour and hasn't produced a puppy, you must call your veterinarian immediately. In some cases the female is unable to deliver by herself and will need the help of your veterinarian. A *cesarean section* operation could be necessary.

After the Birth

If the mother dog doesn't show any interest in her puppies, you will have to clean them and take care of them. Baby puppies cannot urinate or defecate without stimulation. The mother stimulates them to do this by licking them. If for some reason you have to raise the puppies on a bottle, you will need to stimulate them by stroking each one from under the tail to the navel area with a soft, warm, damp cloth or paper towel.

Babies that have to be hand raised can be a lot of work. They might have to be fed as frequently as every two hours, day and night, depending on their size. There are special liquid and powder milk formulas made for puppies. If you have puppies that won't nurse their mother or a bottle, you will need help from your veterinarian.

A Checkup for Mother and Puppies

It's a good practice to make sure that your veterinarian sees the mother and puppies within 24 hours of birth.

The veterinarian can palpate the mother to be sure she has delivered all of the puppies and *placentas*. If she has a retained puppy or placenta, she could die without veterinary help. The veterinarian can also check the mother for milk quantity and quality, check the puppies for deformities, and remove dewclaws if necessary.

The mother dog licks the puppy to stimulate it to urinate and defecate.

Newborn puppies are completely dependent on their mother for nourishment.

CHAPTER

Training and Teaching Your Dog

In order to do a good job of training your dog, it's important for you to understand how a dog experiences his world. You need to know what makes a dog "tick."

The Basic Nature of a Dog: Leader or Follower?

Dogs are pack animals and by nature need to live in a group situation. A dog's position in the pack can only be at one of two levels: the leader or a follower. Except for very rare individuals, dogs really don't care if they're the top dog or not, but they do need to know what their position is at all times. It doesn't take a puppy very long to accept its new human family as its pack. The real question is, will it be a leader or a follower?

If a dog isn't sure whether he's the leader or a follower, he will try to be the leader until you show him differently. Being the leader is a hard job for a dog. If you show him that you are in the number one position, your dog will easily accept being a follower. With that he gets the security of belonging to your pack.

Your Role as Leader

You must be the leader, but you cannot lead with cruelty. You must be firm but fair, understanding and respecting your dog's natural instincts. You must not permit misbehavior, but you also must never be abusive. A dog that is full of fear is unstable and unpredictable and therefore not a good companion.

It will be your goal to direct your dog so that he understands and learns what is acceptable behavior. He can only do this if your training is clear, consistent, and properly timed. I'll cover this further later in this chapter.

The Dog's Senses

A dog has the same senses as a human, but they are different in several ways.

Smell

Your dog lives in a world rich with scents that we cannot even imagine. The part of his brain that receives messages about scents is over 1,000 times larger than ours. Not only can a dog tell the difference between hundreds and hundreds of smells, he can also remember them. And he's able to notice a very small amount of a particular odor, even if there are many other odors present.

A dog can smell the "signatures" of other dogs, as well as many other scents we can't smell.

Your dog can walk through your kitchen while your mom is baking an apple pie. Even though the smell from the oven is strong, he seems to pay no attention. He walks over to you and puts his nose on your shoe, reading just where you've been and what you've walked through.

The dog's sense of smell is so finely tuned that he can pick out your scent on the one object you've touched from all of the others in a pile of identical objects. (See page 137 to learn how to teach your dog tricks that use this talent.)

Sight

The dog's sense of sight is sharp when it comes to viewing familiar shapes and moving objects. His ability to distinguish fine details is not as well developed as that of humans, though. A dog is not good at picking out differences in movement or shape, for example. I've tried walking past dogs that knew me with a limping gait or my hair in a much different style, and they have always acted as if they didn't recognize me until I spoke or they could catch my scent.

Hearing

The dog can hear all of the frequencies that a human can hear — and well beyond. To some extent, dogs are able to move their ears in the direction of the sounds they hear. They tune in to different things in sound than humans do.

Your Dog's Instincts

Instinct. A behavior that an animal is born with and is not learned.

An *instinct* is a behavior pattern that is inherited and not learned. An example is suckling. All mammals are born with the instinct to nurse their mothers. They don't have to be taught to do it. Dogs — including your puppy or dog — have inherited strong instincts from their wild ancestors.

Your pet dog will show some of these inherited instincts. As you live with him, see how many instincts you can identify:

- Guarding: Your dog may guard your yard, your home, or a toy.

- Pack instinct: This is the instinct to group together. If your dog is with several other dogs, he will have the instinct to behave as if he's a member of a pack.

- Prey drive: Prey drive is the instinct to chase a moving object. In the wild, dogs displayed this instinct when they hunted. Herding, driving, and chasing are all parts of prey drive.

- Digging, barking, and marking are natural behaviors of dogs and are familiar to us.

Off to a Good Start

You're about to begin a wonderful experience with your dog. Take your time and learn the proper way to direct your dog and help him to be all that he can be.

Equipment

A soft nylon buckle collar and leash are what you will need in the way of equipment to start out training your puppy. You will add a chain slip collar later, when you begin obedience training.

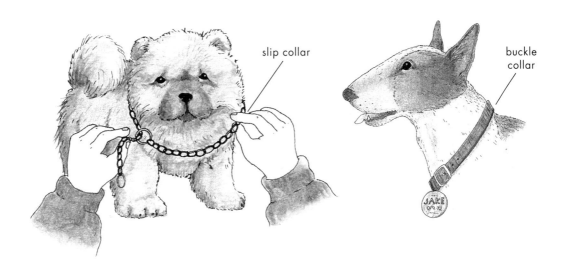

slip collar

buckle collar

The slip collar on the left is safe and useful only when it is properly placed on your dog, as shown in this drawing. Use it only when you are present, your dog is on a leash, and you are holding the leash. The buckle collar on the right is a good choice for everyday wear. Your dog's rabies and/or identification tags can be attached to the ring.

Earning Your Puppy's Respect, Trust, and Confidence

Your dog needs a leader, and that's you. A puppy must learn self-control and self-discipline. He will learn this as you help him to be obedient. The puppy needs lots of affection, but you must not let him have his way when what he's doing isn't right. He will learn to follow your guidance because he wants to be obedient. You teach your puppy obedience by repeating the same thing over and over and giving praise when he gets it right.

Getting the Message Across

Your dog is a thinking creature, but he doesn't think with words the way you do. In order for a dog to understand us, we have to get a message to him in a language he will understand. We do that by showing him what we want him to do, praising him when he does it right, and correcting him when he does something we don't want him to do.

There are certain dos and don'ts we must remember when living with a dog:

- Do praise your dog when he does something you've asked him to do and does it right. Only give praise when the dog earns it.

- Do use treats only for training.

- Don't lose control and get angry or rough with your dog.

- Don't let your dog be confused about who's top dog. Example: Don't let your dog go in or out of a door ahead of you or without your permission.

- Don't play dominance games such as tug-of-war with your dog. This puts you and the dog on the same level and encourages aggression.

Be a Good Citizen

Check out your local laws to see if a license is required for your dog and what immunizations he will need. Check the local ordinances to see if there are any restrictions on dogs in your area.

If you're thinking about taking your dog to a public place such as a playground, park, or nature reserve, check to see whether dogs are allowed.

When you do take your dog out in public, remember that you must accept total responsibility for his behavior. Clean up after him and leave the area better than you found it.

Teaching House Manners

Decide what behaviors you will and will not allow from your puppy. The best way to correct a problem behavior is to prevent it in the first place. Don't put your puppy on your lap while you're on the couch if you don't want him to get on the couch as an adult. Never give the puppy a command that you can't or don't enforce. An example is telling a dog "down" when he jumps on you. Are you going to squat down and put the dog in a down position? Does your dog know the word "down" yet? Is "down" what you really mean, or do you mean "off"? The main thing to remember is that you're trying to communicate with your dog and teach him that you don't want him jumping on you. A better solution would be to say "off," take the dog's feet and remove them from you, and praise him when his feet are on the ground.

Crate Training and Housebreaking

Wild dogs want to keep their dens clean, so they pick toilet areas away from where they live and sleep. Domestic dogs have inherited this instinct from their

Earn Your Dog's Trust

Remember that you should never get angry at your dog, yell, repeat a command over and over, or hit or handle him roughly. You will gain nothing except your dog's mistrust.

wild ancestors. To housebreak your puppy, all you need to do is to reinforce this natural behavior. Housebreaking and crate training go together. The crate becomes your dog's "den." That's why crate training your dog will help in housebreaking him. When you have unruly visitors, his crate is the one place your dog can go (or you can put him) for privacy. Very small children may unintentionally injure or irritate your dog by pulling his hair, tail, or ears. They can walk over his feet and tail, try to climb on his back, and throw objects at him. Your dog has the right to be treated with respect, so the crate is the perfect place for him while they visit.

Crate Training

Crate training is a method of giving your dog a place of his own to sleep, gnaw on a chewable treat, or just get some privacy. The crate feels very much like a den to your dog. When you're going to take your dog with you in a car or truck, or even if you go on vacation, you can take along his crate and he will feel right at home, anywhere.

Your puppy learns quickly that his crate is his "safe" place.

The Right Crate

The first crate for your pup should be just a tiny bit larger than he is. If the crate is too large, your puppy can divide it into a sleeping area and a potty area. When your puppy is reliably house trained, he's ready for a larger crate. Eventually you will need a crate big enough to accommodate the full-grown dog.

Steps in Crate Training

The first few times you work on crate training, your pup should be a little bit hungry. Place a light-colored towel in the crate. Pick a word you will always use when you're going to put the puppy in the crate: "crate," "kennel," "pickles" . . . any word will do. Whatever the word is, your dog will soon understand that it means "go get in your crate." Eventually, you can use that word to tell the dog, from anywhere in the house, to go to his crate — and he will!

Show the puppy a food treat, making sure he's really paying attention. Kneel down on the floor in front of the open crate and hold his buckle collar with one hand. Show the treat again, then toss it into the crate. Give your "get-in-the-crate" word. The dog will run into the crate to get the treat.

Close the door, but leave it closed only for a minute or so. Don't overdo the length of time. If the dog is quiet, give him praise. Don't open the door if your puppy starts pawing or whining. Open the door only when he stops whining or pawing. Opening at the wrong time will reinforce the behavior you don't want.

Let the puppy out, and with another treat repeat the exercise. Over a period of a week or so increase the time he stays in the crate.

Never use the crate as punishment. If you're angry at your dog and want to banish him, calmly put him in the crate, without scolding him. If you scold your dog as you're putting him in the crate, he may be confused. He may think the crate is for jailtime and learn to dislike it, or he may think you're scolding him for going into the crate.

Don't feed your dog in the crate. You can put water in the crate during the day if you must keep the dog confined there for more than a couple of hours.

Always be sure the crate is in an area where there's good ventilation and your dog won't be too hot or too cold. Some short-faced breeds (Chow, Pug, and Boston Terrier, for example) or those with heavy coats (such as the Malamute and other northern breeds) need extra holes drilled in plastic crates so that air will circulate properly.

Maximum "Crate Time" at Different Ages

8 weeks .... 3 hours
12 weeks .... 4 hours
16 weeks .... 5 hours
6 months .... 7 hours
1 year .... 8+ hours

Just because your dog is able to stay in his crate for a long period of time doesn't mean you should keep him in the crate that long.

Housebreaking

The more time you spend with your new puppy or dog, the faster he will learn not to urinate or defecate in the house. A puppy is just a baby and must learn what you expect of him. An older dog may have to learn new habits, depending upon how he was housed and trained before.

What Doesn't Work

You have probably heard someone say, "If the puppy makes a mistake, rub his nose in it," or, "Drag him to the site of the disaster, point at the puddle or pile, and scold him." Don't use either of those methods. They don't work. All you'll do is frighten the pup and make a mess for yourself to clean up. A dog is so upset when he is being scolded that he can't even begin to understand exactly what you're angry about.

Watch for the Signs

Be with your puppy as much as possible so that you can learn his different sounds, body movements, and behaviors. You will soon notice that the puppy behaves in a certain way immediately before he begins to relieve himself. This is a cue for you! Watch for this cue and use it to your benefit. You will have only a few seconds to get the puppy outside to the place you want him to use. Don't scold him if you aren't fast enough.

What Does Work

Pick a spot (in the yard or wherever you choose) that you want your puppy to use as his potty area. Place a piece or two of his stool in that spot. This will act as a cue to the pup. Take him to that spot immediately after eating. Praise him gently the instant he starts to relieve himself. The praise must be quiet and calm. You don't want to get the pup so excited that he forgets what he started to do. When he's finished relieving

When a Mistake Happens

There's often a reason why a housebroken dog makes a mistake. Think carefully and see if you can come up with an answer. Maybe you changed his food. Maybe your dog is sick. Maybe he ate something that he shouldn't have eaten, such as some toilet paper or a houseplant.

himself, shower him with major praise and maybe a few minutes of play in another area.

Don't play with your pup until he relieves himself. If he doesn't relieve himself within 5 or 10 minutes, put him in his crate and try the whole thing over again in 20 minutes or so. Don't forget the praise at the completion of the job.

Clean up the area every day, leaving a small piece behind as a reminder for a few days. Once you're sure the pup thoroughly understands what the potty area is for, clean up the area completely each day.

If your puppy is very small, you may have to carry him to the potty spot. Otherwise, try to take him out wearing a collar and leash. Never let the puppy follow you without any type of restraint. Keep a leash and collar by the door. If you see your pup start to circle and sniff the floor, he's almost certainly looking for a place to potty. You'll have to be fast. Pick him up if necessary, and get him to the potty area.

Confine the pup to a single room at first, preferably one with a tile floor. Put a baby gate across the entrance, if possible. You must be able to observe the puppy when he's out of the crate, so don't lock him in the bathroom. The best time to allow the puppy freedom in this room is after he has properly relieved himself outdoors.

When the puppy is reliable about staying in the crate, staying in the single room, and relieving himself when he's taken outside, you can gradually allow him more freedom in the house. Don't give the puppy too much freedom too fast. He may find a nook or cranny at the other end of the house that he considers a perfect spot to relieve himself. Go slowly with your puppy and you'll have a more reliable pet.

Nighttime Potty Breaks

If you're very lucky, your pup will sleep through the night. But if he doesn't, he will need to be taken outside once during the night. Your parents might want to handle this one responsibility for you. This is a rough time for both of you. Your puppy needs to relieve himself during the night because his bladder isn't large enough for him to wait until morning. In a few weeks, this will pass.

If possible, don't wait until the puppy is whining continuously to be taken out. This could cause a whining problem you will have to correct later. Try to get up when you hear the puppy stirring restlessly and before he whines. Take him outside, on the leash and collar, straight to the potty spot. Don't act impatient or the puppy might think he's doing something wrong. If he relieves himself, praise him calmly. If he doesn't

Training Schedule for a 10-Week-Old Puppy

*Playtime can follow any potty break
or be part of free time*

6:30 AM	Upon awakening, potty break.
7:00 AM	Breakfast, followed by potty break — put out water. Free time in one room.
9:30 AM	Potty break. Nap in crate, followed by potty break.
12:00 PM	Lunch, followed by potty break. Free time in one room.
2:30 PM	Potty break. Nap in crate, followed by potty break.
6:00 PM	Supper, followed by potty break. Free time in single room.
7:30 PM	Pick up water bowl until morning.
9:00 PM	Potty break, followed by bedtime.

relieve himself within the normal length of time, take him back to his crate, put him inside, and go back to bed without a word.

Housebreaking Tips

Whenever your pup or dog is loose on the floor, spend as much time as you can with him. If he starts to relieve himself, lift him gently and carry him to the potty area. Don't yell at your dog, no matter what happens and no matter how much you have to clean up. Here are a few tips to keep your puppy on a fairly regular schedule:

- Feed only dry food until the puppy is house trained. Canned food has a high moisture content and added chemicals that can affect the frequency of your pup's urination.

- Feed on a regular schedule. Take the puppy out immediately after each meal.

- Watch for the puppy to awaken from a nap. Take him out right after a nap.

- Take the puppy out between meals and naps so that he doesn't go more than two hours without a potty break.

- Take the pup out first thing in the morning and last thing at night.

Paper Training

Some people prefer to use the paper training method of house training. This is convenient for apartment dwellers and for those with little access to an outside area. The puppy is confined to a small area in which the whole floor is covered with newspaper. This should be a noncarpeted area. Since the whole area is covered, the puppy will have no choice but to relieve himself on the paper.

No Nighttime Treats

Never, ever play with the pup or give him any food or treats during this nighttime potty break. Resist any attention other than the praise. The pup must not think nighttime is a time for recreation and socializing.

Paper training is often the only house-training alternative. Remember, though, that any newspaper or magazine lying on the floor could be a "target" for your dog.

After several days, begin removing some of the paper. The puppy has become used to the idea that he should relieve himself on the newspaper, and he won't eliminate on the area of the floor that's bare.

Eventually, you might use a large litter pan or plastic blanket box with a paper liner in the bottom. Once the puppy is dependably eliminating in the litter pan, you can gradually give him more access to the house. Some people don't use the litter pan method, but without a litter pan, the dog may think any paper object on the floor is a fair target. I know one dog whose aim was so accurate that he used a *TV Guide* that was on the floor.

Housebreaking Problems

Here are some common housebreaking problems, and suggestions for dealing with them.

Excited Urination

Dogs that are on the submissive side may squat or lie on their sides or backs and urinate when they get excited. This usually happens when they first see you or even a stranger. It's hard to believe, but this is a compliment from the dog. He's telling you that you're much higher on the ladder of importance than he is. He's also saying that you have his devotion and he will look to you for direction. Most dogs grow out of this, but occasionally a very submissive adult will continue this through his life. Sometimes it helps to teach the dog games such as retrieving that build self-confidence. The act of leaving you and going out after the toy is the key factor here. The dog is making a decision to leave your side and pursue an object he wants to catch.

Marking

If your dog urinates on your bed, your dad's shoes, or your sister's umbrella, he's trying to let everyone know he's claiming that territory. This dog is confused about just who is in control in the house. You need to straighten him out. This rarely happens with a dog under eight months of age, and nearly always happens with a male. Females may mark before, during, and after they come into their heat cycle, however.

If marking is caused by *hormones,* neutering or spaying the dog will usually cure the problem. I recommend neutering or spaying before the dog is sexually mature.

If marking is a *dominance* issue — the dog is confused about who is in charge — a few brush-up lessons on the leash will remind him that he is not the dominant member of the family. If he hasn't had basic obedience lessons, it's time to get started, right away. Either way, if you use a firm, fair hand in training, the dog will normally stop the behavior. This also works on males in some toy breeds that are notorious for marking if they are not neutered.

Hormones. A substance that is produced by one of the organs in an animal's body.

Relieving Himself in the Crate

If your puppy or dog urinates or poops in his crate, here are some possible causes and suggested solutions:

- The crate is too large. Get a crate that's just slightly larger than the dog so that when he's lying down, he covers nearly all of the floor.

- The dog or puppy was previously kept in a crate, possibly with a wire bottom or papers in it, and expected to relieve himself without going for a walk or outside. If this is the case, begin to take the dog out for walks to the potty spot very frequently. Give extra praise when he relieves himself outside.

- You're leaving the dog in the crate too long. Get him on a shorter schedule.

- The puppy is sick. Your veterinarian might wish to check for urinary infections or disorders or an upset in the digestive system. There is a defect in some dogs that causes leakage of urine when the bladder gets partially full.

- The puppy or dog won't relieve himself in the potty area and then does relieve himself in his crate when you bring him in. Have you ever caught your dog in the act of relieving himself where he shouldn't have been doing so? Did you scold him? The puppy may think that you don't want him to relieve himself at all, so he waits until you're out of sight to do so.

Solving Behavior Problems

Puppies and dogs can develop some behaviors that we don't like. Before you can find a solution, you must understand why your dog is acting this way.

Afraid of the Stairs

If your puppy will gallop up the stairs, and then stands at the top and refuses to come down, he's normal! Puppies are rarely afraid to go up stairs, because their balance seems to be fine in that direction. But when their head and front feet are headed down, they feel off balance, as if they're going to tumble down.

Solution: Put the puppy just two stairs from the bottom. Call him to you or show him one of his favorite toys or a tiny piece of his favorite treat. The puppy should easily master this short distance. Praise him with great zest. Gradually, over a period of many days, increase the number of steps until he has mastered them all. Be very careful, however, because stairs can be dangerous to puppies if they tumble.

Pups love climbing up stairs, but may need training to learn how to come down.

Begging

This is one problem behavior that is created by people. Never give your dog treats when you're eating. No matter how much you would like to share your lunch with your dog, don't let his big brown eyes sway you to give in. Once you've started to give the dog food when you're eating, he will be relentless in begging from you and even other people. Your dog should receive all of his meals in one place or the same dish. Treats should be reserved for play and training times only.

Solution: If your dog has already developed this habit, you will have to resort to scolding him for something he now thinks is fine with you. If your dog is already obedience trained, you could use the "stay" command when you try to retrain to stop the begging. When the dog begs, say "no!" and take him a reasonable distance away where you can still watch him. Put him at a "stay," even facing away from you. If the dog breaks the "stay" and still tries to beg, repeat the same procedure. You must be consistent and do this no matter where he starts to beg. Putting the dog in the crate won't give him the correct message. Your dog won't learn that begging is no longer "legal" in your house. The crate shouldn't be used for punishment.

If your puppy learns it's okay to beg at the table, you may find his behavior very irritating later, when he's an adult.

Jumping Up on People

Dogs jump up on people to get attention. Puppies should be taught from a very young age not to jump. The main key in preventing and stopping jumping is not to give the puppy or dog any type of positive attention when he does jump. Don't pet him or talk to him in a way that he might misunderstand as approval.

Allowing a dog to jump up on people will eventually backfire and cause you trouble. The dog might be muddy and get someone's clothes dirty. The person may have arms full of groceries, including eggs and breakable bottles. The person may be elderly or handicapped. In any case, it's not a good behavior to allow.

Solution: If your puppy is young enough, use a stern voice to say "off!" as you take his paws off you and place them on the ground. Then praise the dog. If you see that the puppy is coming over and has that "I'm going to jump on you" look, give him a firm "off" before he jumps and you'll be one step ahead. As he sits down, praise him. For a large dog, you can take a small step forward as he approaches and lift one knee to block him from full body contact, at the same time giving him a stern verbal "off." The minute he sits down, praise him.

For a dog that is resistant to the mild solutions above, I suggest that he be taught the "sit" command covered in the obedience section on page 118. As the dog approaches, give the "sit" command and praise as he sits.

Chewing

All dogs, especially puppies, love to chew. Dogs naturally pick up and carry things in their mouths. The chewing desire is with a dog all through his life, but is strongest when he's teething, from about 5 to 10 months of age.

You can teach your puppy that only items from his own box are okay to use as play toys.

Is Your Dog Eating His Toys?

Some dogs are prone to *pica* — the behavior of eating and swallowing things that are nonfood items. Pica is rare in dogs, but you should always watch what your dog does with a particular item. If you find that he is eating a particular material, such as plastic, rubber, or paper, eliminate those materials when you are selecting toys for your dog.

Solution: Collect a selection of chewing items that are safe for the puppy and "legal" for use in your home. Things you can buy include rawhide and nylon chew toys, knotted ropes, Cresite hard-rubber balls and tugs, and various other dog toys. Place all of the "legal" chewing items in a tub or box. Make sure the puppy knows that anything that isn't from this box is off limits. (See page 121 for more on your dog's toy box.)

Keep the box handy so that when the pup starts to chew on Mom's favorite chair, you can redirect his chewing urge. Scold only when you catch him actually chewing on something that's off limits. Tell the pup "no chew" in a firm voice as you hand him a "legal" item to chew. Praise the pup when he takes the item.

Keep your eyes on the puppy when he's free in the house, until he's well past the critical teething stage. Don't stop watching him until you're sure that chewing is no longer a threat.

Whining

Whining can become an irritating habit if it isn't corrected immediately. Spending too much time with your puppy can cause him to be overly dependent on you. He needs to learn to accept being alone, or without your attention, even if you're home or in the same room. Your dog may also whine when he needs to go out or when he's hungry.

Solution: If it's near the time the puppy needs to relieve himself, take him right out to the potty area. Return him to the same spot when he's finished.

If the dog is in his crate, be sure he has some toys to keep his interest. You don't want the puppy to think he's banished or being punished when he's in the crate.

If the puppy isn't in the crate, watch his body language when he whines. Is he trying to get your attention because he needs your help? Maybe his chew toy was taken by another dog or is behind a closed door.

Barking

Dogs bark for several reasons:

- They sense danger.

- They want something they can't get by themselves: food, water, a toy, a cat in the neighbor's yard, another dog.

- They're annoyed or bored.

- They're joining other dogs in song.

Solution: The first two reasons for barking can be corrected by changing the situation. In the case of the last two reasons, don't allow the dog to bark for so long that it becomes a habit. These are usually problems of an outside dog that has little interaction with his family. Such barking is irritating to almost anyone who hears it, and can cause problems between your family and your neighbors. A barking dog wants attention. Give him plenty of attention. Play fetch, or take him for a healthy jogging expedition before you go to bed. Both of you will sleep more soundly.

Whining for No Reason

If you can't find any reason for the whining, ignore it completely. When it stops, you can take the puppy out of the crate and play with him. Never remove the puppy when he's whining, or you will reinforce the whining and it will continue — only stronger next time.

Getting into Garbage

This is a problem created by putting tempting tidbits in the garbage and expecting your dog to ignore them. Remember, a dog's nose rules his head.

Solution: Empty the garbage often or keep it out of reach.

Digging

This is most often a problem with outside dogs that are bored. When you spend a lot of quality time with your dog, he won't be interested in digging. Dogs dig for several reasons. Terrier breeds were developed to dig out their prey. Other dogs have this instinct also, but to a lesser degree. All dogs have a keen sense of smell and can identify animals, insects, and even certain objects that are under the ground. They'll dig to get to the item.

A dog digs to make a den.

Solution: Provide a doghouse or other "den."

A dog digs to find cool earth to lie on and cool his body in hot weather.

Solution: There should be cool spots in the dog's pen.

A dog digs for fun and out of boredom.

Solution: If you give your dog plenty of attention, he's less apt to be a digger.

Escaping

A dog that's loose and out of control can cause huge problems for you, for other people and their property, and for domestic and wild animals. Escaping is also dangerous for the dog.

Solution: Before you ever leave your dog alone in the yard, check every inch of the fence and gates to make sure that there's no way the dog can find an escape route. Once a dog discovers that he can get out of the yard, he will continue trying, even if you repair every place he finds. Check for loose, rusted, or broken

A Pen of His Own

If your dog must be outside for long periods of time, he should have a pen of his own, within the yard. (Page 29 tells you how to set up your dog's pen.) This will prevent unwanted digging behavior in other areas.

wire; cracked or rotted wood; easily opened gate latches; and gaps between the fence and the ground. Make sure that the fence is tall enough to prevent your dog from jumping over, and that it's constructed of a material that will keep your dog from climbing out. If the fence wire isn't buried in the ground, the dog may dig under it. The best way to cure escaping is to prevent it in the first place.

If the dog is continually left alone and isolated, he will become restless and bored. Dogs are intelligent; they know that the grass is greener on the other side if they aren't getting much attention at home. Also, if they aren't neutered, both males and females will go to all lengths to escape and find a mate. Neutering is a must for dogs that aren't going to be used for breeding.

Lots of play and exercise will satisfy and tire the dog and reduce the chances that he will search for a way out.

Mouthing

Mouthing is a dog's habit of putting its mouth on people and other dogs. It's natural for puppies, but it isn't pleasant to people. Puppies need to do a certain amount of mouthing of each other to learn just how hard they can bite in play. But you're not a puppy, and you shouldn't allow your puppy to bite or mouth you. This would put you on the same level as the puppy, as if you were his littermate. As he gets older, he may think he can be dominant over you.

Solution: If your puppy bites, even in a light way, give a loud, convincing "ouch!" response. If he stops mouthing or biting, or tries to lick your hand, praise him. If he doesn't, repeat the "ouch!" at the next bite. If the puppy doesn't seem to get your message that the biting is painful, grab his muzzle and say "no!" the next time he bites. If he stops, praise him and give him a chew toy. You must be consistent and never give up. The puppy will eventually learn the lesson.

Eating Poop (Coprophagia)

Although it's disgusting for us to realize our dog has done it, this is a natural behavior for dogs, and common among many animal species. In today's world, it isn't a healthy practice for the dog and it's not healthy for us to be around a dog that does this. Parasites and diseases can be easily transmitted by this behavior. Puppies are prone to this problem a little more than adult dogs are.

Solution: If you have more than one dog, put each one in the potty area separately. Clean up every little speck before you let the dog with the problem enter the area. Stay with him every minute, and scold him with a firm "no!" if he makes any attempt to eat his own feces. There are also products you can add to the dog's food or put on the feces that are said to stop the practice.

Chasing

Chasing is another natural behavior for dogs. Dogs also use the chase behavior in play. They love to chase and be chased.

Solution: Don't play chase games with your dog unless you both have been through at least basic obedience training, and you have pretty good control of your dog.

A dog can only chase a cat that's running away.

Solution: If you wish to introduce your puppy to a cat, be sure that the cat isn't afraid of dogs and is quiet natured. You should have some light obedience control on the puppy before you begin an introduction. With the puppy on-leash, introduce him to the cat. If the puppy isn't gentle with the cat, give him a verbal "no!" and a light correction with the leash. If you allow him to be rough with the cat or move toward it too fast, the cat may run; that will increase the chances that the

Chasing Cars

Dogs have the instinct to chase things — including, sometimes, cars. The car is "running away" from the dog, and if he barks at the car and "chases it off," he feels like the winner. Your dog should never be loose and able to do this.

puppy will want to chase it. If you have a cat that isn't socialized with dogs it will be difficult, if not impossible, to keep the cat from running away. And the running will stimulate the chase.

Leash Training

You will need to train your puppy to walk with a leash attached to his collar as soon as possible, so that you can take him to relieve himself. Start out with a soft buckle collar. Let the puppy get used to the feel of it.

Next, attach a short leash to the collar, and let the puppy get used to dragging it around. You must always be within sight of the puppy when he's dragging a leash, because it might get caught and tangled. You can play with the puppy while he drags the leash by putting a little tension on its end.

Now pick up the leash and follow the puppy. If the puppy is obstinate, show him a treat and put light pressure on the leash as you try to guide the puppy to walk on your left side. If he does a good job, reward him with a treat. Don't drag, choke, or force the puppy into perfect position. All you want at this stage is for the puppy to get used to being restrained with the leash. Once he is, you can use the leash whenever you work with your puppy.

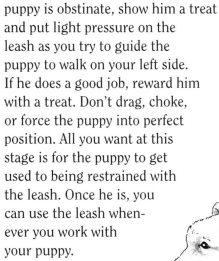

Manners and obedience training will teach your dog that you are taking him for a walk, not the other way around.

Obedience Training

If at all possible, enroll your puppy or dog in an obedience class. If you're a member of the 4-H Dog Group, obedience could be part of your program. Also check with local dog obedience clubs and your local Humane Society.

Training should be a happy time for both you and your dog. If your dog is treated harshly, he will be afraid or will resent the training sessions. Your dog must eventually understand that he must mind you. Most dogs are followers looking for someone to lead them. Your dog will learn to respect you by the way you treat him and the way you reward him when he has done something that you like.

Sometimes you can unintentionally reinforce undesirable behavior in a dog by saying something in the wrong tone of voice. If the meter reader comes up to the fence and your dog is barking and barking up a storm, and you say — in a nice tone of voice — "Now, that's okay, he's a friend," what your dog is hearing is, "It's good that you're barking. You should always bark at that person." If you want the dog to stop doing something, you must always get his attention first, by calling his name. Then tell him that you don't like what he's doing. Be as simple as possible, with something like: "Sandy, no bark." What the dog understands is, "I don't like what you are doing. Don't do it." A simple "good dog" in a voice that's pleasant is sufficient to let the dog know he has done something that has pleased you.

There are countless methods for teaching a dog obedience. The method I'll describe in this book is the most pleasant for both trainer and dog. You will use treats as rewards at first, but eventually you will get the response you want from your dog for praise alone. Your goal is for your dog to work for praise and loving. He will soon learn when you're getting ready to teach him something new.

For the sake of description, I've named the imaginary dog in the next section Maple.

Training Tip

The relationship between you and your dog will depend on trust, fairness, firmness, and repetition. It's important to understand that you won't be able to teach your dog something that isn't a natural thing for him to do. You can't teach your dog to pick up a pencil or telephone with one paw the way you do with your hand, because it isn't physically possible for the dog to do it.

Attention

Before you can get your dog to learn something new, he must be paying attention to you. To get your dog's attention in early training, you must make it worth his while.

Attach a leash to your dog's collar. Hold the leash in your left hand. Face your dog and put a tiny treat between your right thumb and index finger. Say, "Maple, watch me." Stroke the treat along the dog's muzzle, past his nose, and up to the outside corner of your right eye. If the dog makes eye contact with you, quietly tell him, "Good dog," and give him the treat. Repeat this several times. Soon, you'll be able to eliminate the stroke along the muzzle to your eye; your dog will give you eye contact just with the command, "Maple, watch me."

Stay

This a very important obedience command to teach your dog. If you ever see your dog entering a dangerous situation, such as crossing a busy road, you'll be happy you taught this.

With the dog in a sitting position, tell him "stay," give a slight backward pressure to the leash, and pivot in front of the dog so you are facing him. Praise your dog if he doesn't move, then pivot back to his side. Repeat this several times, eventually lengthening the time and distance you are away. When the dog has mastered this in the sit position, you should teach him to stay in the down position using the same method.

Attention: Use a treat to teach your dog to make eye contact with you. Soon he will automatically look to you for directions. Praise him when he does it right.

Stay: When you tell your dog to "stay," your hand should look like a solid barrier in front of his face.

Sit

The sit can be easily taught with a treat and a little physical help. Your puppy should be in a relatively calm mood to teach him the sit. With him standing in front of you and facing to your right, show him the treat, say "Sit," and move the treat to his nose and slightly over his head, at the same time lightly pushing down on his rump. If the dog sits, immediately give him the treat and praise. Keep the praise calm so that you can repeat the exercise several times. Within a few tries, the dog will sit without the push on his rump. Then you can tell him "sit" and not offer the treat until he does. This usually takes only one lesson to learn. If possible, try to have several practice sessions in one day.

Sit: When you teach your puppy to "sit," hold a treat above his nose and use light pressure on his rump. Don't forget to praise him when he does it right!

Heel

Obedience should always be taught with the dog
walking on the left side of the handler. Since your dog
already knows how to walk on a leash, you can easily
teach him that "heel" means to stay next to you
without pulling or lagging on the leash. A good place
to teach this to a puppy is along a wall or fence, where
he won't have an opportunity to wander. Don't crowd
him too much, however, or he may begin to lag
behind or forge ahead.

Start out with the dog in a sitting position next to
your left side. Tell him to "heel" and start off with
your left foot, which will act as a cue. Also, give a light

Heel: Teaching your
dog to "heel" along a
fence or wall helps
keep him moving
straight ahead. Be
sure there's ample
space between your
dog and the fence so
he doesn't feel
squeezed.

tug on the leash. Praise the dog as he stays next to you. Every time you stop, tell your dog to "sit" — assisting him, if necessary, with a slight pressure on his rump with your left hand and a slight upward movement with the leash with your right hand. Don't forget praise for everything your dog does right. When he has mastered the "heel" this far, add changes in your speed and direction, and circle around objects.

Come

An important thing to remember is that when your dog misbehaves, you should never call him to you and then punish him. No dog in his right mind would come a second time!

Once your dog has learned to walk on the leash, put a longer line on him and let him wander and explore. Give the command "come" and lightly tug on the leash. If the dog comes toward you, lavish him with great amounts of praise and even a treat. If the dog is confused or resistant, reel him in to you without being forceful, and praise him. Soon you can run with the dog on a long line and let him play. At unexpected times, give the command "come" and praise the dog if he does. If he comes without the need for a tug, give him a treat also.

Down

Ask your puppy to sit, with the leash hanging down from his collar. Give the command "down," stroking with a treat in your right hand from his nose and down his chest to the ground. At the same time, lightly tug the leash toward the ground. If the dog resists after several tries, you may need to lift his front paws from under him with your left hand while pulling down with your right. Don't forget to praise and give a treat.

Having Fun with Your Dog

The best part about having your own dog is that you can have so much fun with him. There are many games and tricks you can play together. Sometimes your dog will play by himself, too. A dog that is busy playing and learning doesn't have a lot of time to get into trouble trying to figure out something to do.

Your Dog's Toy Box

Place all of your dog's toys in a tub or box. Teach the pup that this box belongs to him, and it's full of fun! Give the box a name, like "the box." Get the puppy interested in its contents by rummaging around in it. Talk with an excited voice, picking up one toy and then the next. Show them to the pup, then toss them back into the box and get some others. The puppy will soon begin to explore his new box. If he finds something he likes first, praise him; otherwise, hand him a toy and then praise him.

Toys

A vast array of playthings are available for dogs. You can find some good ones in stores. You can also make great toys by recyling stuff from around your house.

Shoes Are Not Toys

It is not a good idea to give your dog old shoes to play with. The dog will have a hard time telling the difference between the old shoe you give him and one you want to wear.

Old Socks

You can give your dog old socks to play with. If you tie a knot in the middle, he can learn that the only "legal" socks in the house are the ones that have knots in the middle. Knotted socks are great for playing fetch or for the dog to toss around by himself. When the socks get dirty, throw them in the laundry and return them to the dog.

Dog Frisbees

Dog Frisbees are made of either hard nylon or a softer, flexible material. They can take tough treatment from a dog's teeth, and are easy for him to pick up with his mouth.

Chewing Items

Your dog is a born chewing machine. The urge to chew is extremely powerful in puppies in their teething period, when they're four to eight months old. But dogs of all ages enjoy having their own items to chew.

Edible Chewing Treats

Dogs can't floss or brush their teeth the way we can. Instead, nature has provided them with the urge to chew things that will help remove tartar from their teeth and keep their gums healthy. This chewing urge is especially strong in puppies that are replacing their baby teeth with the teeth of an adult dog. The new teeth that are coming in put pressure on the puppy's gums and baby teeth. Chewing helps loosen the baby teeth and make room for the new teeth.

Chewing is an enjoyable pastime for dogs. If they have something "legal" to chew, they might keep away from shoes, socks, table legs, and carpets. Puppies, in

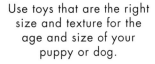

Use toys that are the right size and texture for the age and size of your puppy or dog.

particular, must satisfy their chewing urge when teething. If you don't supply them with safe items to chew, they might choose an object that isn't safe for them, or one that's valuable to someone in your family.

Rawhide Bones

Pet stores offer a wide variety of edible chew treats in a vast array of shapes, sizes, and flavors. Rawhide bones are made of beef hide shaped into bones, rolls, chips, sticks, and strips. They also come in a half-dozen flavors such as "savory beef gravy," "irresistible peanut butter," "real hickory smoked," and more. There are also ground and pressed rawhide bones and sticks that a dog can chew up more quickly.

Specially Treated Real Bones

Specially treated real beef bones are made from knuckles and long bones. The bones are sterilized. Some are smoked for extra flavor. These are especially good for larger dogs, although they start at about 3 inches long and go up from there, all the way to a 16-inch bone that weighs 3 pounds.

One of the latest natural chew products on the market is made from by-products of meatpacking plants. Cow ears, pig ears, muscle chews (made from a muscle and ligament in the necks of cattle), and sliced cow hooves make chew treats that hardly any dog can resist.

Natural Bones

Certain natural bones can be given safely to dogs, but only if you follow these suggestions. Ask your butcher to cut beef shank bones and knuckles into sizes appropriate for your dog. It's important that each bone is cut all the way through at some point so that you can remove the *marrow* later.

Real Bones Are Dangerous

As a rule, most real bones are unsafe for puppies or dogs, because they can splinter into sharp pieces. The dog's nature is to swallow even these dangerous pieces of bone, which can cause serious problems inside his body. It's possible for a dog to swallow nearly any bone that will fit into his mouth. Never give your dog steak, lamb, pork, or chicken bones.

Raw bones begin to have a very bad odor as bacteria grow on them, so they should be cooked as a health precaution. Cooked bones don't seem to develop this problem as quickly.

Place the bones in a pot large enough to hold them along with enough water to cover them completely. Cover with the water, and add about 1 teaspoon of minced garlic or 2 sliced garlic cloves per gallon of water. Bring to a boil and let simmer until the meat particles come away from the bones easily. You may have to replace some of the water as it boils away. Turn off the burner and let it cool on the stove. Never try to move the pot of boiling liquid until it's cool.

When it's cool enough, put some of the bones in another container and take them to the sink. Now you can easily remove the marrow from inside each bone, as well as any meat or residue that could stain carpet or clothing.

Wash the cooked bones thoroughly, scrubbing with a brush. Line an open baking pan with foil. Put the bones in the pan in one layer. Roast in the oven at 250°F overnight. You can prepare enough bones at one time for many portions for your dog. Package and freeze any you aren't going to use immediately.

Chewing Items — Nonedible

There are many nonedible products that will satisfy your dog's natural urge to chew.

Nylon

Chew bones, disks, and tugs are made from a nylon material that helps stimulate your dog's teeth and gums. They come in two textures: hard and chewy. If your dog is an aggressive chewer, try the hard type.

Corn-Based Formula

Bone-shaped chews made from corn-based material come in an assortment of sizes, colors, and flavors. These are actually edible, but it will take your dog a long time to finish one.

Knotted Cotton Ropes

These come in a variety of sizes. Some dogs enjoy playing with a piece of cotton rope that's 12 to 18 inches long after several knots have been tied in it.

Hard-Rubber Chew Toys

There are tugs, bones, solid rubber balls, and rubber balls with bells in them. The Kong and the Tuffy are chew toys that promote exercise and quick reflexes, because they bounce in unpredictable directions. All of these toys are practically indestructible.

Specially designed nylon and hard rubber chew toys massage your dog's gums and help to curb unwanted chewing behavior.

Playtime

The time your puppy or dog will be anxiously awaiting each day is the moment when you drop everything else to have fun with him. Try to set a regular time to play with your dog, even if it's only 10 or 15 minutes. Don't make playtime the first thing you do when you come home, however. Your dog has been waiting all day while you were at school, and will be terribly excited when you arrive. Always greet him calmly, even if you'e very excited to see him.

 If you come home and give your puppy a great deal of attention immediately, or start right out with playtime, he will become impatient and full of expectation if you're even a few minutes late. Walk in and greet the puppy calmly and basically ignore him for at least half an hour. This might be a great time for you to get your homework finished or do your regular daily chores.

Playtime is very important to both of you. It helps form a bond between you and your dog. Puppies and dogs are really athletes at heart, so games such as fetch are excellent choices. Avoid playing with your puppy in ways that make you look like a puppy, though. Crawling around on the ground and wrestling with him could give him the wrong idea. This could make him feel that you're an equal, like one of his brothers and sisters. He could learn to play rougher with you as he grows older, and try to be the top "dog" of the two of you. The puppy is your friend and your student, but he must never think he's dominant over you.

Exercise can be fun for you and your dog.

Games and Tricks

Once you've trained your dog in basic obedience, you can begin to teach him some tricks. By then he will have learned to look to you for direction, and will pay attention to you when you ask him to do something. The younger the dog, generally, the easier it is for him to learn. You can play games or tricks with your dog for exercise, to stimulate his brain, or for the sheer fun of it.

The Importance of Treats

Some dogs will do almost anything for treats. Remember that the treats you give shouldn't be so filling that they will spoil the dog's regular meals. Sometimes it isn't what the dog is receiving as a treat that's important: What matters to the dog is that you're happy with him, and that he's going to get praise and something special from you.

Training Treats Dogs Enjoy

- Cheerios, tiny cheese crackers, Chex and Kix cereals, plain popcorn, and even pieces of their dry food.

- Chicken or turkey hot dog treats: Slice chicken or turkey hot dogs into small coins. You should get at least 30 from one hot dog. Place on a paper towel on a microwave-safe cookie sheet, and microwave for 6 to 9 minutes. Watch to be sure they're not getting too brown. They should be dry and crisp. Pat out any extra oil, cool, and put in a plastic bag in the refrigerator.

- Liver treats: Liver treats are for very special occasions. Preheat your oven to 300°F. Cut up 1 pound of beef liver or 1 pound of chicken liver and place in a blender. Mix until pureed. Then blend in a bowl with 1 cup cornmeal, 1 cup whole wheat flour, and 1 tablespoon garlic powder. Don't add any salt. Spray a cookie sheet with Pam and spread the mixture over the sheet. Bake until it's dried out. When it's still warm, but not hot, cut into very tiny pieces — no larger than ½ inch square. Store in a plastic bag in the refrigerator.

Beginner's Tricks

Here are some tricks you can teach your dog as soon as he knows basic obedience.

Roll Over

Ask your dog to lie down. Give the command "roll over," and help him to roll over with your hands. Praise him even if you had to help. Give him a treat. Repeat this several times until the dog understands what "roll over" means.

Shake Hands

Tell your dog to "sit." Reach down, take hold of one of his paws, and lift it gently. Raise the paw to about the dog's chest level and tell him, "Shake hands." Praise him. Repeat this several times. Over the next few sessions, give the dog the opportunity to move his paw before you lift it. If he makes even a small move, praise him.

Shake hands: Be very gentle when you lift your puppy's paw. Praise him if he does not resist.

Wave

Once your dog has learned to "shake hands," he's ready to learn the wave. When the dog is sitting, tell him, "Shake hands." Wave one hand at him and say, "'Bye-bye." Touch the dog's raised paw lightly and say, "Bye-bye," again. Praise the dog as soon as he makes the proper effort.

Sit Up

Ask your dog to sit with his back in a corner. Take a treat and hold it just out of the dog's reach. At the same time, give the command "sit up." Starting with the treat just above the dog's nose, raise the treat as he tries to get it. When his front feet are at about chest level, give him the treat and praise at the same time. Repeat several times, making the dog sit up for a slightly longer time. Don't forget the praise.

Sit up: Use a corner to help teach your puppy to "sit up." Keep the treat just high enough over your puppy's nose so that when he reaches for it he will rock back and be in the correct position.

Jump

Put two bricks or other low objects 3 to 4 feet apart on the ground. Place a broom handle from one brick to the other. With your dog in the heeling position, and on a leash, move quickly toward the broom handle. Just as you reach it, give your dog a light tug on the leash and say "Jump." Praise if he doesn't balk. If he knocks over the stick, don't scold; just try again. Eventually you will wish to raise the jump higher, but this should be done very slowly, and not at all for young puppies.

Jump the Stick

Follow the same procedure for the jump, above, but instead of using a broom handle, use a piece of ½-inch PVC pipe. Wrap the pipe with electrician's black tape so that it looks like it's striped. Once your dog can reliably jump over the pipe when it's set about 6 to 12 inches high, take the end of the pipe in your right hand and hold it in front of him about 6 inches off the ground. Ask your dog to "jump," and give a slight tug on the leash. If he doesn't understand after a few tries, go back to setting the stick on the bricks until he realizes that the striped pipe is for jumping over. If he still doesn't understand, ask a friend to hold the stick, and then ask your dog to "jump."

Jump the stick: As you and your dog approach the stick, give a light tug on the leash and say, "Jump."

Jump through the Hoop

If you have an old hula hoop lying around, it can become part of a trick for your dog. Wrap it the same way you did the "stick," above. Start by teaching your dog the regular "jump" trick. Once he knows this well, start all over with the hoop resting on the ground. Ask a friend to hold the hoop. Be sure the friend is on the left side of the hoop. As your dog jumps through the hoop, you will need to collect the leash on the other side so you won't get tangled. Eventually you will be able to trust your dog off-leash to jump through the hoop, but always be sure you're in a fenced yard.

Catch the Treat

Place your dog in a corner, facing you. Show him the treats in your hand. Say, "Catch it" as you toss a treat toward him. If he doesn't catch the treat, don't let him eat it. Repeat this until the dog gets the idea. Eventually you will be able to stand some distance away from the dog to throw the treat.

Carry

This trick is the basis for another trick to follow. Ask your dog to open his mouth. Put an object in her mouth. (A 6- to 12-inch wooden dowel is a good object to use for this training.) Hold his mouth closed for a few seconds, release, remove the object, and praise the dog. Repeat this only once or twice at a time, because the dog will tire of it quickly. Practice often. When he will hold the object without spitting it out, put a little pressure on the leash to make him step forward. Eventually, you will want your dog to come all the way to you, carrying the object from several feet away.

Carry: Touch the wooden dowel lightly to your dog's front lips and teeth as you say, "Carry." Praise him when he takes it.

Fetch

If your dog knows the "carry," you should have little problem teaching the "fetch." Many dogs are natural retrievers and don't need formal training for the "fetch." However, if your dog is one that runs after an object but doesn't pick it up, or picks it up and heads away from you, he will need training. He should already know basic obedience and the "carry" before you start to teach him the "fetch." When you teach the "fetch," your dog must be on a long line and willing to work with that restriction.

Throw a ball and tell your dog to "fetch." If he runs after the ball and picks it up, repeat the "carry" command and give a light tug to bring him to you. Praise him and repeat several times.

If the dog runs out but doesn't pick up the ball, calmly walk up to him, pull his head lightly down to the ball, repeat the word "fetch," and, if necessary, lift the ball to his mouth. Repeat the "carry" command, giving a light tug to bring the dog to you. (You must walk backward a few steps.)

If you throw the ball and the dog does nothing, you will have to repeat the command "fetch" and walk the dog out to the ball, pull his head lightly down, repeat the word "fetch," and, if necessary, lift the ball to his mouth. Then repeat the "carry" command, tugging lightly to bring the dog to you. (You must walk backward a few steps.) Don't be rough with or talk sharply to your dog. He's learning, not being disobedient. If you get angry at your dog, he will learn nothing.

Advanced Tricks

Please master all of the beginner's tricks before you try the advanced tricks. They help your dog understand that if he works hard, he will have a lot more fun than he would just being a couch puppy.

Crawl

Give your dog the command, "Down." Don't let him turn over on his side, the way many dogs do when they lie down. This is a time to use one of your dog's very favorite food treats. Hold the treat just out of reach of his mouth. Put your other hand over his shoulders in case he tries to get up. Tell the dog, "Crawl," and start moving the food away. If he tries to stand up, your hand is there to prevent it. If you don't move the treat too far too fast, your dog should crawl a little, even if it's just an inch or two. Praise and let him have the treat. Gradually increase the distance.

Say Your Prayers

Ask the dog to sit, facing a chair. The chair must be of the right height and weight for your dog's size. If the chair is too light, it might slip. If your dog is small, try using a small stool. As the dog sits, lift and place his front feet on the chair. Reassure him that this is a special trick and you're pleased he isn't fighting you. Gently lower his head to his paws so it looks like he's praying. Keep the reassuring up because this is a very unnatural position for a dog. Praise the dog if he doesn't move. If he does move, you could add the "stay" command. Repeat this several times per session until the dog does it on his own with the command, "Say your prayers."

Prayers: With your dog sitting and facing the chair, place his paws on the chair. Praise him and gently push his head to his paws. Use a treat as encouragement if necessary.

Dance

When your dog knows the sit-up trick very well, slowly raise the treat much higher over his head. Ask your dog to "Tango," or whatever dance you choose. As he gets to his feet to reach the treat, praise him and give it to him. Repeat this several times so the dog knows that when you say, "Tango," he should stand on his hind feet. When he's standing solidly upon that command, move the treat slightly to one side so he must take a step or two, making a one-quarter turn. Praise and give the treat. Don't try to go too fast with the dance trick. Gradually move the treat a little farther, until the dog is turning halfway then all the way around before he gets the treat. Within a short time you will only have to say, "Tango," and move your hand over his head in a circle, and your dog will swirl around one, two, three times.

Dance: Hold a treat just out of your dog's reach so that he stands up on his hind legs. Gradually, over several sessions, teach him to turn by moving the treat in a small circle so that he follows it by moving his hind legs.

Nose Soccer

Put a ball directly in front of your standing dog. Place a small treat just behind the ball. Move the ball so your dog sees and eats the treat. Repeat this several times. Soon he will push the ball away to get the treat.

Take the Paper to Mom or Dad

Your dog already knows how to "carry." Ask one of your parents to hold the long line. Roll up the paper and ask your dog to "carry." Then say "Take it to Dad," or "Take it to Mom." Your parent gives a light tug on the line to bring the dog closer, then gives him a treat. If you wish to have this be a family trick, the dog can be taught to bring any reasonable object to any family member. He will soon learn the names of all of the family members, especially if they all have treats.

The Seal Act

This trick is done with a special treat because the dog must balance the treat itself on his nose — like a seal! Ask the dog to "sit" and place the treat on the very top of his *nose leather*. Hold his *muzzle* for a few seconds, telling him to "wait." Take the treat, put it in the dog's mouth, and praise.

Repeat this procedure two or three times. The fourth time, don't put the treat in the dog's mouth; merely release your hands. If the treat falls, grab it before the dog gets it. The reward will be eating the treat.

This takes a lot of patience from both of you. Sometimes the treat is so fragrant that the dog will drool while he is "holding." As the dog progresses in this trick, make him wait even longer after you release your hands — up to 20 or 30 seconds. When the dog is successful at this trick, you might want to try moving his head so that his nose is pointing at the ceiling. Place the treat on the end of his nose. All the time, remind him to "wait." The treat for this trick should be truly special as a reward for your dog's self-control.

Seal act: Put a treat on top of your dog's nose and hold his muzzle for a second or two. Tell him to "wait." Then take the treat and place it in your dog's mouth.

After your dog has learned to let the treat sit on his nose while you hold his muzzle, take your hand away and tell him to "wait." After a few seconds, give him the treat.

Find It

The dog has a marvelous nose and can use it for finding hidden treats, toys, other objects, and people.

Hidden treats. Take one treat and hide it in a very obvious place, such as just barely under the edge of a throw rug. Tell the dog to "find it." Take him to the rug, point to the hiding place, and flip the rug over a bit as you repeat, "Find it." Often a dog will beat the trainer to the punch by smelling the treat first and finding it on his own. Next, with the dog looking on, place another treat under a different part of the rug. Repeat the command, "Find it." Let the dog try to find it by himself. Don't forget to praise him if he's successful. Now put the treat behind a chair where the dog can easily find it without destroying something and repeat the command, "Find it." You can practice this outdoors, also.

Hidden toy. Repeat the same training method as in the hidden-treats trick above, but use the dog's very favorite toy. When the dog finds it, play with him and the toy as a reward.

Find it: Use a treat with an irresistible odor to teach this trick. Remember to praise your dog immediately when he finds it.

Pick the right object. Cut 10 or 12 sticks, each about 12 inches long. Since you have just handled them, place them in a container and let them sit outside in the air for at least 24 hours. Take one of the sticks and play fetch with the dog. Then dump all of the sticks out of the container, without touching them, in a loose pile. Place the stick you've just been handling on top. Tell the dog to "find it" (not "fetch"). Watch as your smart dog finds the stick you've just handled. You can use other objects instead of sticks. They don't all have to be exactly the same.

Hide-and-seek. Once your dog has mastered the other "find it" games, you can teach him to find a person who's hiding. When the dog finds the person, both of you should reward him with a play session.

Exercise

Dogs are natural athletes and love to run, jump, and play. You can begin with light exercise even when your puppy is eight or nine weeks old. Dogs shouldn't be allowed to jump obstacles until they're mature, however. The impact on their legs and shoulders when they land will hurt their growing bones and joints.

Water exercises put little stress on a dog's bones, and dogs seem to thoroughly enjoy them. Once you have taught your dog to "fetch," you can play the same games in the water. If you do this in a swimming pool, watch your dog carefully so that he doesn't get hurt jumping in. Some dogs get so excited that they seem to throw safety to the wind. Also, remember not to leave your dog in the pool, because he may not be able to find his way out. A tired dog could drown in a very few minutes.

Here are a few things to remember before exercising your dog:

■ Never overdo exercise with your dog. He may enjoy being with you so much that he doesn't recognize how tired he is until he drops from exhaustion.

Dog Puzzles

Try to invent games that will challenge your dog's thinking abilities. Put a treat in an open cottage cheese container, for example, and let him figure how to get it out. If that's easy, you can try something harder, such as a closed cottage cheese container, a cardboard box, or an upside-down laundry basket. Lots of storage containers have openings in their sides and one side open. Place the treat on the floor with the container over it so that the dog can see the treat. Let him figure how to get it out.

Keeping Fit

Exercise such as walking and running helps keep your dog's body and heart fit, and burns off extra calories that could turn into fat. A fat dog will have a shorter life span than a fit dog.

Your dog will enjoy joining you in all your activities.

■ Plan your dog's exercise program to fit:

His age: Young dogs require exercise of a type and duration that won't hurt their growing bodies. Older dogs may need shorter playtimes and less strenuous exercise.

His body type: Tiny dogs or dogs with shorter legs have to run harder to achieve the same distance as taller dogs.

His condition: Check with your veterinarian before you start an exercise program with a dog that's overweight or not in peak condition.

The weather conditions: Dogs can get overheated rapidly in hot weather. In cold weather they can get overheated, and then get chilled very quickly when they stop. This is especially true of short-coated dogs.

Start exercise routines slowly and keep them short. If your dog ever acts tired, stop for that session.

Check the pads of your dog's feet to be sure they are tough enough for the surfaces you will be playing on. Recheck the pads when you're finished to be sure there are no injuries that must be treated.

Be sure water is always available, but never let your dog drink too much at one time after strenuous exercise. If your dog gets so thirsty that he gulps down huge quantities of water, he may vomit it all up, along with his previous meal.

Activities for You and Your Dog

Talk to your parents if you are interested in looking into dog-related activities that are away from your home. If they tell you it's okay for you to look into one or more of these activities, here are some places to check out. (The addresses for some of these organizations* are found in "Helpful Sources," later in this book.)

- Your county extension service — Ask about 4-H programs with dogs.

- The chamber of commerce of your city — Ask if they know of any dog training groups.

- American Kennel Club* — Ask for any dog clubs in your area.

- Mixed Breed Dog Club of America* — Ask where the nearest events are held.

- American Mixed Breed Obedience Registry* — Ask where the nearest events are held.

If you enjoy traveling and working with your dog and like to be around other people with the same interest, there are many dog-related activities from which you can choose.

Volunteer

You might want to become involved by volunteering to help in the dog-related activities that suit your interests before you actually begin training in them. This way you can see if it's what you really want to do. You could become a dog show steward or judge's helper, for example. You will learn a lot by being the right hand of the judge. You might also be assigned to do the physical work of moving jumps, changing equipment, getting handlers and their dogs lined up, handing out ribbons, cleaning up, and anything else that there is to do.

During this volunteer period, you can watch how the handlers and their dogs work together. Ask questions. Pick times when the handlers you admire aren't busy.

Types of Activities

Some activities are only for purebred, registered dogs. Some are for mixed-breed dogs only, and some are for all dogs.

If your dog is especially athletic and willing to learn, you have a wide variety of activities from which to choose. You will then need to learn how to train and motivate your dog so that he can master the skills necessary for the sport you select.

Dog-related activities are grouped into the following six categories:

- Training and learning experiences
- Conformation shows and matches
- Obedience trials
- Performance events
- Noncompetitive events
- Service dogs

Get Information

Sometimes a dog event fits into more than one of the above categories. Before deciding on any one activity, try to attend a wide variety of these events, so that you can get a "feel" for which ones suit you and your dog's abilities the best. Most of these activities require long hours of dedicated training. It's better to start slowly and with a goal that's realistic for both of you.

When you have found a dog sport that interests you and is within the capabilities of you and your dog, find out more about it. Read everything you can find about it. If you're able to connect to the Internet, you can find lots of information there. (See "Helpful Sources.") Talk to people who are already participating in that sport. Ask how much time they feel is necessary to put into training and practicing. See if there's an organized group that practices and helps newcomers.

Once you have found out all of this information, you can begin to decide whether you have the time and dedication necessary to train your dog in this activity. It's so exciting to see a well-trained and successful dog-and-handler team perform in any of these events. But it takes hours, days, weeks, months, and sometimes even years of training to reach that level.

Active dogs are great for active kids.

Make Sure Your Dog Is Prepared

When you travel to training sessions and events, you must make special provisions for your dog. Both you and your dog should be in good physical health and able to withstand the physical and mental strain that will go hand in hand with the training. Stress caused by

changes in schedule could affect you and your dog.
Here are some important requirements:

- Your dog must be crate trained.

- Your dog must be well socialized with other dogs
  and people.

- Your dog must be manageable on a leash and collar.

- For some activities, your dog must already be
  obedience trained.

- You must take food and water from home. Changes
  in diet and even water can affect the dog's system.

- You should ask your veterinarian ahead of time for
  medicine for travel sickness and stress-caused
  diarrhea, just in case you need it. Get all of the
  instructions on how to use it in writing.

- You should keep your dog crated and in a quiet place
  when it isn't necessary for him to be out. New situations are very exciting and tiring for a dog. Cover the
  crate with a light cloth to promote rest and privacy.
  (If your dog has a heavy coat and the weather is warm,
  you may not be able to cover the crate.) If you're
  outside, be sure the crate is protected from the sun.

- You must be calm with your dog, even if it seems
  like he didn't learn anything or he didn't perform
  well. Sometimes it takes several sessions just to get
  a dog used to a new environment. In any case,
  always remember that you started this to have fun
  with your dog. Try to keep it that way.

- You should try to keep other dogs or people away
  from your dog's crate, where he may feel protective
  and vulnerable. He can become exhausted and upset
  if he is constantly worrying about invaders.

- You must not train so hard or long that you or your
  dog gets burned out.

4-H

Whether you live in the city, the suburbs, or the country, there's a 4-H club in your county offering a wide variety of projects for kids and dogs.

The projects are geared for kids and dogs from beginning through advanced levels. Different clubs offer different projects. Besides basic dog care and training, some clubs have projects for training Seeing Eye dogs, guard dogs, or advanced obedience.

Cost

There's little or no cost to members for 4-H activities. Local 4-H clubs are staffed by volunteers and sponsored by the Cooperative Extension Services. Members are required to have the proper equipment for their dog (usually a leash, collar, crate, etc.), along with immunization and de-worming records.

4-H Goals

"Learn by doing" is the 4-H slogan. In 4-H dog projects, kids learn by working with their own (or a borrowed) dog.

"To make the best better" is the 4-H motto. Being a part of the 4-H dog program will give you a chance to make one of your best friends, your dog, the best he can be. You will learn to how to teach him to become a good citizen, with good manners. You will learn how to take care of him by learning about proper nutrition, grooming, and health and exercise issues.

Age Requirements

Kids can start in 4-H as young as 6 years of age and stay until they're 18. Children in the "Clover" group (six to eight years of age) are allowed to participate in all matches and shows, but on a noncompetitive basis.

Breed Requirements

All breeds of dogs are welcome in the 4-H program, including mixed breeds. There's no discrimination against dogs with handicaps. In some areas, there's a much higher percentage of mixed breeds.

Meetings

4-H groups meet at least once a month. Some groups may meet as frequently as once a week. Each meeting offers a learning topic, fun activities, and social time with other members.

Record Book

Part of 4-H is learning how to keep information about your dog activities in a record book. The book might cover training, exercise, expenses, and feeding. You could even win an award for the quality of your record keeping.

Projects

Projects in 4-H can cover a wide variety of subjects, such as nutrition, health care, grooming, obedience training, body structure, conformation showing, correcting bad habits, and even tricks.

Projects can be ongoing from year to year. You can see the progress you make with your dog. He becomes a good citizen in your community and you both are happy.

Shows

4-H project leaders may hold practice shows, called matches, during the year so that everyone can see how far they have progressed and where they need extra work.

One or two times a year, shows are held at the district level; there, 4-H clubs with dog projects from several counties gather to compete. It's a great opportunity to meet kids your age who are interested in the same things you are.

Once a year, a large show is held on the state level, where all 4-H dog project clubs compete. Competition classes at these shows are usually conformation, obedience, showmanship, musical obedience, and drill (team competition). The Clovers may enter and earn participation ribbons, but they don't actually compete for placements until they are older.

Community Service

In addition to meetings, matches, and shows, 4-H dog groups are usually active in community service. They visit people at nursing homes and orphanages. They are invited to be part of parades as a group, walking or riding on a float.

Competitive Events

In these events, dogs are shown against one another to see which is the best in that class or category on that particular day. Established standards and rules are followed in each type of event. One or more judges place the dogs in the order they qualify. In timed events, the judges also look for faults or flaws that affect the score.

Preparing for Competition

The first thing you must do is learn all of the rules that apply to a particular event. Some rules might seem pretty unimportant, but they allow the judges to score each performance according to the same standards. Never be angry at your dog if you don't win. Some judges will disqualify you if you treat your dog roughly.

Don't Forget the Fun

It's fun to be in a competitive event with your dog. If you win a prize or ribbon, it can be very special. The important thing to remember, however, is that you started this all for fun. No matter how your dog scores or places, he must have fun. Otherwise, your dog will feel less motivated to perform next time.

Dogs entered in show competition must be trained to stand properly and quietly, yet they must still have a happy attitude. You can use small pieces of cooked liver or other treats to get your dog's attention, and as a reward for standing well. Judges look the dog over completely, even in his mouth, and run their hands over the dog to feel his body condition and structure.

Conformation Shows and Matches

A conformation show is a beauty pageant for dogs. Some U.S. dog shows have over 3,000 dogs entered on a single day. There's also a huge show called the World Dog Show, which is held in a different country every year. It lasts four to six days and can include over 10,000 dogs from all over the world.

At conformation shows, judges evaluate the structure, appearance, and movement of the dogs according to a standard of perfection for that breed of dog. This standard of perfection is called the breed standard. It tells what the dog should be like down to the finest detail. It includes things such as eye color and shape; coat color, texture, and length; number of teeth and how they fit together; shape of the head and other body parts; size and weight; ear type and placement; attitude; movement; and bone structure. The standard also tells what would disqualify a dog, including color, missing teeth, and temperament.

In a conformation show, you present your dog in the best way possible.

Conformation shows are held only for purebred, registered dogs. These events are put on by all-breed clubs such as the AKC and UKC, or breed-specific clubs such as an all-Poodle. They are held to give points to winning dogs toward earning a championship.

A match is very similar to a regular conformation show. It's mainly for practice and experience. The dogs get ribbons and placements, but they don't earn points toward a championship.

Junior Showmanship

In these classes the handlers are between 10 and 16 years old. The handlers (not the dogs) are judged for their expertise in showing their dogs. This event can be divided into as many as six classes, by age and experience, including novice classes for entrants who haven't yet won three times. Some experienced junior handlers are so proficient that they are hired to show other people's dogs in regular conformation shows.

Obedience

Obedience classes are divided into Novice, Open, Utility, and Tracking. They can be held by multiple-breed clubs, single-breed clubs, and mixed-breed clubs. Each class has a specific set of exercises for the dog and handler to perform. In all of the classes (in AKC competition) except Tracking, the judge scores the dog and handler by deducting for each mistake (made by either dog or handler) from a possible high score of 200. A score of 170 is necessary to qualify. Three qualifying scores are necessary to earn the titles Companion

Groomed for Competition

For conformation and junior showmanship classes, both the dog and the handler must be well groomed. The dog must be groomed to perfection. The junior handler should wear comfortable shoes, and clothing that's appropriate and in good taste. It must allow the junior handler free movement and the ability to run and bend over when necessary. At no time should the handler's clothing overshadow the dog.

A dog must stay at the "sit" for one minute in Novice class and three minutes in Open class.

Dog (for the Novice class), Companion Dog Excellent (for the Open), and Utility Dog (for the Utility).

There are hundreds of obedience training groups in the United States. There might be one in your area. Check with your county extension agent to see if there's a 4-H program for dogs nearby. This program includes some obedience.

Novice

In the Novice class, the dog must heel with the handler both on and off leash. He must stay in a sitting position when directed to do so, and come to the handler when called. He must stand quietly for examination by the judge. He must also stay in position twice — once sitting, once lying down — with the handler across the ring. Three qualifying scores are needed to earn the title Companion Dog.

Open

The dog performs all of his exercises off leash. These exercises include a heeling pattern, dropping to the down position at the handler's command, two retrieves of a dumbbell (one of which is over a high jump), jumping over a broad jump and returning to the handler, and staying in position twice (once sitting, once lying down) with the handler leaving the ring. Three qualifying scores are necessary to earn the title Companion Dog Excellent.

Utility

Utility is the highest level of the three obedience classes. The dog must perform a directed retrieve, respond to hand signals, and pick out its handler's scent on one article in a group of similar articles. The latter is done twice, once with leather articles and once with metal. The dog must also jump over an obstacle indicated by the handler with a hand signal. Three qualifying scores are necessary to earn the Utility Dog title.

Tracking

Tracking (following a scent) is also considered an obedience event. There are currently two levels of tracking: Tracking and Tracking Excellent. Both are performed outside in a field. A tracking course is laid out, with appropriate turns and cross-tracks, and is aged according to the level of the test. (A new tracking test under consideration is laid out over variable surfaces, such as both grass and pavement.) In all instances, the dog must follow the track, in a line, without the assistance of his handler.

Performance Events

There's a great variety of performance events for dogs. Some of them are for particular types of dogs, such as racing hounds, scent hounds, or herding dogs. They may or may not be sanctioned by dog clubs. Some are sanctioned by an organization formed for that particular sport. Most are competitive; others are just for the fun of it.

Coursing and Racing

These performance events are geared toward the sight hound breeds such as the Greyhound, Whippet, Saluki, Rhodesian Ridgeback, Borzoi, Irish Wolfhound, and Basenji. (See chapter 1, pages 11–12, for more information on sight hounds.)

Coursing is a sport that comes naturally to racing breeds such as the Greyhound, Whippet, and Saluki.

Coursing is a sport that imitates the ancient sport of hunting rabbits by using sight hounds to chase them. Today a special lure course is set up in a field, with a line threaded around several pulleys that are staked to the ground. At the far end of the line is an artificial lure that takes the place of the rabbit. The dogs run unleashed after the lure as it's pulled through the course.

Jack Russell Terrier Races

Running these feisty little terriers is a popular sport among horse show enthusiasts during horse show intermissions. The terriers run from starting boxes. A piece of fur tied to a line is used as a lure. The doors to the starting boxes all open at the same time, and the dogs chase the lure down a field and through an opening in a wall of baled hay. The first dog through the opening is the winner. Some of the races are on flat ground; others are over hurdles. They are also part of Jack Russell Terrier shows.

Herding

This event is performed by a distinct group of breeds originally developed to collect, herd, drive, and separate livestock, such as sheep, cattle, goats, and ducks. (There's more information about herding dogs in chapter 1, page 11.) A few other breeds also participate, but they may use the hunting instinct to "chase" these animals, rather than actually herding them.

Well-trained herding dogs respond to verbal, whistle, and hand signals.

Agility

This sport is fun for both the handler and the dog and is enhanced by the way they work together. The handler/dog team has a set amount of time to run through a course of brightly colored obstacles and equipment. The dog works off leash at the direction of his handler. Some of the obstacles include a pipe tunnel, a board walk, a collapsed tunnel, an A-frame, various jumps, weave poles, a seesaw, a tire jump, and a pause table. The dog must be physically fit. There must also be excellent communication between the handler and the dog. Points are deducted if the dog makes a mistake.

Most breeds can run agility courses, except those that are very large or wide. The breeds that seem to be best suited to agility are medium-size, naturally agile, fast-paced dogs such as Border Collies, Australian Shepherds, retrievers, some terriers, and mixed breeds.

Sporting Dog Trials

A special and unique relationship must develop between a hunting dog and his handler. The two must work as a team, each counting on the other to do his or her part. One of the events at sporting dog trials consists of the dog working the ground in a zigzag pattern until a bird (usually a pheasant) is flushed. At that point, the dog freezes in position and waits until the hunter shoots the bird. The dog must watch exactly where the bird falls, and must not move until his handler directs him to retrieve the bird. The handler uses whistle commands during the trial to tell the dog which direction to move, or to halt.

Flying Disk or Frisbee

This sport is spectacular, and exciting to the spectators as well as the participants. The dog catches a flying disk thrown by his owner. Dogs in this sport have developed talents that are incredible to watch. They seem to fly

Check These Out

Some other performance events you might want to learn about are:

- Flyball
- Musical Freestyle
- Performance Art (tricks)
- Go-to-Ground or Earth Dog Trials

through the air, sometimes doing flips as they catch the disks. In formal competition there are three levels. The Timed Toss and Catch level gives the dog-and-handler team 60 seconds to make as many catches as possible. The distance of the catch, as well as whether the dog jumps into the air, remains partly on the ground, or remains totally on the ground, determine the scoring. In the Novice Freestyle level, a team has 90 seconds to perform using a maximum of 10 disks. There are a number of required moves that must be included, but the team may add others. In the Advanced Freestyle level, the time limit is two minutes, and the required moves are more difficult.

Sledding (Mushing)

Sled dogs have been used for decades in the North Country to move people and their belongings across vast areas of snow and ice. While sled dogs are still used for work, teams of them also compete in races now. Today's sled dogs come from Alaskan Malamutes, Siberian Huskies, Eskimo dogs, and several other breeds with Nordic heritage. Many are the result of crosses with other medium- to large-breeds; Greyhound heritage is found in some sled dogs used for racing. The teams are almost always four or more dogs.

The Iditarod

A famous sled dog race called the Iditarod is held annually to commemorate the 20 drivers and their valiant dogs that ran, in relay, a distance of nearly 700 miles across Alaska in five and a half days in temperatures of -40°F. Their accomplishment saved the lives of many people, because their precious cargo was serum for a diphtheria epidemic then raging in Nenana, Alaska.

Sledding is a popular sport in northern states.

Weight Pull

Dogs of any size can be trained in the weight pull; however, the dog should be at least one year old, to prevent damage to growing bones and joints. You shouldn't use heavy weights until your dog is fully mature. In this event, a dog is trained to wear a special pulling harness that distributes the weight to the proper parts of his body. A special line attaches the harness to a sled or flat cart. At a trial, there are classes based on the dogs' weight. Each competes in his own weight group. Each dog in the group has the opportunity to pull the starting weight. Those that accomplish this pull can compete in the next section, in which more weight is added. The dog that pulls the most weight in a class is the winner.

Noncompetitive Activities

Some of the following activities can also be practiced in competition, but many owners are involved in them just for the fun of it. Dogs are used for a wide variety of sports other than those listed in this book; you may even invent some of your own. But here are a few more.

Carting

Carting is often performed at specialty shows for the larger draft-type breeds of dogs. Medium- through giant-size breeds are best suited for this sport, although I have heard of some small breeds shown in exhibition with miniature carts. In draft-type carting, a harnessed dog or team of dogs pulls a wagon or cart. The dog is usually led by a leash. Exercises differ, but usually include the dog standing still and waiting as the handler opens a gate, then traveling through the opening and waiting again as the handler closes the gate; traveling through a narrow opening; backing up; and more. Weight is not the issue, but rather how well the dog maneuvers through and around various obstacles.

Sulky carting with a dog looks like a miniature version of a horse pulling a sulky. The dog wears a bridle and a small harness, to which the shafts of the cart are attached. The cart has one or two bench seats. The driver sits on the front seat and drives the dog with the reins. Voice commands may also be given for direction, speed, starting, and stopping.

Dog Runs

Clubs and organizations may hold a dog run in your community to benefit a favorite charity. They are often called "fun runs," because they're only mildly competitive; there may be winners in various categories, but the prizes are usually small. A fun run is a race in which owners run or walk with their dogs over a marked course. I have participated in fun runs where some people made matching costumes for themselves and their dogs. I even saw one where the person was dressed like a dog, and the dog was dressed like a person.

There is usually an entry fee. All participants receive back tags with their entry numbers, along with some sort of item to commemorate the event.

Skijoring

This sport began in Scandinavia, where there's a lot of snow. The handler must be a good skier, and the dog must already be trained to pull. Basically, the dog wears a pulling harness and a long line that's attached to a special belt around the person's waist. The dog pulls the person on skis, following the commands for direction, speed, and stopping. This sport can be dangerous if either the handler or the dog isn't experienced.

Hiking and Backpacking

This activity utilizes the strength of your dog to carry packs strapped over his back while you hike together. Some breeds are better suited to this sport than others;

however, most dogs that are healthy and fit can carry at least one-third of their body weight in backpacks once they have been properly conditioned. This means that a 60-pound dog could carry 20 pounds. Dogs shouldn't carry fully loaded backpacks until they are fully mature, though; a dog under one year of age should carry only empty packs, or packs with very light loads. The packs must be of even size and weight and have a good strapping system.

Train near home at first, until you are sure your dog can travel the time and distance you expect on your first trip together.

You and your dog can go hiking together.

Community Service

There are many organizations in your community that would welcome you as a volunteer. If your dog is good with all kinds of people, has proper manners, and is properly trained, you might be able to perform some special services for your community. Be certain that your dog has been acclimated to a wide variety of people, places and situations. An adult who is familiar with the dog should always accompany you.

Humane Society

If your parents agree, check with your local Humane Society about its volunteer program. Each society may have a different program.

Volunteers can help with the care, feeding, walking, grooming, and socializing of puppies and kittens. Volunteers usually have to attend an orientation session and pay a small fee. Each volunteer is asked to make a commitment for a set length of time.

Hiking Guidelines

- Check with the proper authorities before your trip to see if the hiking area prohibits dogs or contains animals that your dog may want to chase or that might want to chase your dog.

- Treat your dog for fleas and ticks.

- Don't let your dog eat or drink anything he may find on your hike.

- Keep your dog on leash, quiet, and close to you.

- Always clean up after your dog and yourself.

Local Libraries

Libraries are always looking for new and interesting presentations to include during their summer and vacation programs. Here are some suggestions you might like to offer to your librarian.

- Show the other children what your dog has learned from your training. After you show them what your dog can do, give a brief demonstration on how you trained him to do one or two things. You could have one session on obedience, one on manners, one on tricks, and so on.

- Demonstrate and talk about how you take care of your dog: feeding and grooming.

- Prepare a little skit or play, or just show off the tricks you have taught your dog.

Nursing Homes

Nursing homes often welcome visitors that have gentle, well-groomed, and well-trained dogs. Be sure to first visit the nursing home with a parent and without your dog to get its approval. The residents get a very welcome break from their daily routine and have the opportunity to watch you and your dog have fun together. The dog should have met all the health, temperament, and training criteria. If you're interested in your dog becoming a certified therapy dog, see the "Helpful Sources" section for an address to write for more information.

Show-and-Tell at School

You may be able to fit your dog into a program or report for one of your classes. Sometimes teachers have a day when children can bring their pets to school. Always be certain that your dog is clean, well groomed, and well mannered, and fits all of the criteria for taking him into a public place. Remember to take a crate along so your dog can rest after his performance.

Requirements for Community Service

- Your dog must be well groomed, current on all inoculations, parasite free, and in good health.

- Your dog must be well trained in basic obedience.

- Your dog should have been trained to go potty while on the leash.

- Your dog should be good with individuals or groups of strangers of different ages, sexes, races, and activity levels.

- Your dog should not beg for food.

- Your dog should be of moderate temperament and not overactive.

- Your dog should not lick everyone he meets or everyone who talks sweetly to him.

- Your dog should not be overly sensitive to distractions, including loud or unusual noises.

- Your dog should not object to being touched by an unfamiliar person.

- You should have thoroughly tested your dog in situations in which there might be loud noises, unusual movements, strange odors, wheelchairs, and people with unusual gaits.

- Your dog should be crate trained.

Traveling with Your Dog

A trip with your dog can be in the car around the block or on a plane for hundreds or thousands of miles. Here are a few tips to help make the trips fun and trouble free.

Get your dog acclimated to traveling. Start out with a very short ride in the car. Take the dog's crate, and one or two of his favorite playthings. Load the crate into the car and teach your dog to enter the vehicle only upon your command. If he already knows the "crate" command, it will be easier for him to understand what you want him to do. After a few trips, your dog will need little encouragement once he hears the car keys jingle. Once the dog is crated, and the car

First-Aid Kit for Beginners

- Sterile gauze pads

- Vet-wrap nonadhesive bandage

- Disinfectant

- First-aid spray

- Adhesive tape

- Tongue depressors for a splint

- Blunt scissors to cut tape

- Soap to clean wounds

begins to move, give him time to figure out what's happening on his own. Make the trip short and sweet; maybe a drive to a nearby park. Don't let the dog get out of the crate until you give him the "okay" command. Clip the leash on the dog, then let him get out of the crate. If the distance from the car to the ground is high, help the dog down so that he doesn't receive a heavy impact on his front legs when he touches the ground.

Dogs may get carsick due to anxiety or to actual motion sickness. Making the trips short, fun, and happy will usually eliminate this problem. If nothing seems to help, ask your veterinarian for medical advice.

Wherever you go with your dog, please remember proper etiquette: Clean up after him, don't allow him bother other dogs or people, and keep him comfortable and safe.

Try to keep your dog on his regular schedule for food and exercise.

If you're traveling for a longer period of time, pack all of the things necessary so that your dog will feel at home: food, water, dishes, toys, crate, bedding, collar, leash, grooming supplies, plastic bags for poop, his license, and a first-aid kit. A beginner's first-aid kit should include only items you know how to use properly. Other items may be added as you learn more about treating injuries or problems.

Appendix

Recognized Pure Breeds
American Kennel Club

Sporting Dogs — 24

Brittany
Pointer
Pointer, German
  Shorthaired
Pointer, German
  Wirehaired
Retriever, Chesapeake
  Bay
Retriever, Curly-Coated
Retriever, Flat-Coated
Retriever, Golden
Retriever, Labrador
Setter, English
Setter, Gordon
Setter, Irish
Spaniel, American Water
Spaniel, Clumber
Spaniel, Cocker
Spaniel, English Cocker
Spaniel, English
  Springer
Spaniel, Field
Spaniel, Irish Water
Spaniel, Sussex
Spaniel, Welsh Springer
Vizsla
Weimaraner
Wirehaired Pointing
  Griffon

Non-Sporting Dogs — 16

American Eskimo
Bichon Frise
Boston Terrier
Bulldog
Chinese Shar-Pei
Chow Chow
Dalmatian
Finnish Spitz
French Bulldog
Keeshond
Lhasa Apso
Poodle, Miniature &
  Standard
Schipperke
Shiba Inu
Tibetan Spaniel
Tibetan Terrier

Herding Dogs — 16

Australian Cattle Dog
Australian Shepherd
Bearded Collie
Belgian Malinois
Belgian Sheepdog
Belgian Tervuren
Border Collie
Bouvier des Flandres
Briard
Collie
German Shepherd
Old English Sheepdog
Puli
Shetland Sheepdog
Welsh Corgi, Cardigan
Welsh Corgi, Pembroke

Working Dogs — 20

Akita
Alaskan Malamute
Bernese Mountain Dog
Boxer
Bullmastiff
Doberman Pinscher
Giant Schnauzer
Great Dane
Great Pyrenees
Greater Swiss Mountain
  Dog
Komondor
Kuvasz
Mastiff
Newfoundland
Portuguese Water Dog
Rottweiler
Saint Bernard
Samoyed
Siberian Husky
Standard Schnauzer

Hounds — 22

Afghan Hound
Basenji
Basset Hound
Beagle
Black and Tan
  Coonhound
Bloodhound
Borzoi
Dachshund
Foxhound, American
Foxhound, English
Greyhound
Harrier
Ibizan Hound
Irish Wolfhound
Norwegian Elkhound
Otter Hound
Petit Basset Griffon
  Vendeens
Pharaoh Hound
Rhodesian Ridgeback
Saluki
Scottish Deerhound
Whippet

Terriers — 25

Airedale
American Staffordshire
Australian
Bedlington
Border
Bull
Cairn
Dandie Dinmont
Fox, Smooth
Fox, Wire

Irish
Kerry Blue
Lakeland
Manchester, Standard
Miniature Bull
Miniature Schnauzer
Norfolk
Norwich
Scottish
Sealyham
Skye
Soft-Coated Wheaten
Staffordshire
Welsh
West Highland White

Toys — 19

Affenpinscher
Brussels Griffon
Cavalier King Charles
  Spaniel
Chihuahua
Chinese Crested
English Toy Spaniel
Italian Greyhound
Japanese Chin
Maltese
Manchester Terrier, Toy
Miniature Pinscher
Papillon
Pekinese
Pomeranian
Poodle, Toy
Pug
Shih Tzu
Silky Terrier
Yorkshire Terrier

Miscellaneous

Anatolian Shepherd
Australian Kelpie
Caanan Dog
Havanese
Lowchen
Spinoni Italiani

Helpful Sources

When you write to these groups, please make sure that you keep your letter clear and state exactly what information you need. Ask if there's a charge and, as a courtesy, enclose a self-addressed, stamped envelope. Normally a #10 envelope folded up inside your letter with one stamp will be sufficient.

Organizations

American Kennel Club
5580 Centerview Drive
Raleigh, NC 27606

United Kennel Club
100 East Kilgore Road
Kalamazoo, MI 49001

Continental Kennel Club
P.O. Box 908
Walker, LA 70785

States Kennel Club
P.O. Box 389
Hattiesburg, MS 39403-
0389

**American Mixed Breed
Obedience Registry**
P.O. Box 7841
Rockford, IL 61126-7841

**Mixed Breed Dog Club of
America**
c/o Chris Dane
100 Acacia Avenue
San Bruno, CA 94066

**United States Dog Agility
Association** (Agility)
P.O. Box 850955
Richardson, TX 75085-
0955

**American Sighthound
Field Association** (Lure
Coursing)
Kathy Budney
1098 New Britain Avenue
Rocky Hill, CT 06067

**American Working
Terrier Association**
(Earth Dog)
Patricia Adams Lent
503 NC 55 West
Mount Olive, NC 28465

**Humane Society of the
United States**
2100 L Street, NW
Washington, DC 20037
(202) 452-1100

**National Association for
Search and Rescue**
4500 Southgate Place
Chantilly, VA 20151-1714

**Musical Canine Sports
International** (MCSI)
Bonnie Bakosti
Box 145
Mount Lehman, BC V4X
2P7, Canada

**Flying Disc Dog
Association**
1471 LaSalle Street
Burton, MI 48509

**Delta Society Pet
Partners Programs**
289 Perimeter Road, East
Renton, WA 98055

Therapy Dogs, Inc.
P.O. Box 2786
Cheyenne, WY 82003

Therapy Dogs International
719 Darla Lane
Fallbrook, CA 92028-1505

**National Disaster Search
Dog Foundation**
323 East Matilya Avenue
#110-245
Ojai, CA 93023-2740

International Weight Pull Association
8130 SW Sorrento Road
Beaverton, OR 97008-
  6817
Bill Kanable
Membership Chairman

Canine Freestyle Musical Canine Sports International
16665 Parkview Place
Surrey, BC V4N 1Y8,
  Canada
Sharon Tutt
Membership Chairman

Additional Reading

You may find that the following books will give you some of the information you're looking for.

The American Kennel Club. *The Complete Dog Book*. New York, N.Y.: Howell Book House, Inc.

Wilcox, Bonnie, DVM, and Chris Walkowitz. *The Atlas of Dog Breeds of the World*. Neptune City, N.J.: TFH Publications.

Information on the Internet

If you are involved with computers at home or at school, you may eventually be introduced to the Internet. Right now, there are great Internet sites for 4-H groups and for many of the activities I have mentioned in this book. You can even get very specific and look only for 4-H groups active with dogs, or only for dogs that do water rescue.

In addition, you will find many pet-chat groups, divided into age groups, including whatever age you are today!

Glossary

anal glands (n.). Special sacs in the anus that deposit the signature scent of a dog.

anus (n.). The external opening to a dog's rectum.

ash (n.). The residue, including minerals, that is left after burning.

bitch (n.). A female of the dog family.

bite (n.). The way the top and bottom teeth mesh together, especially the incisors.

blue-blood (n.). A term sometimes used for a pure-bred dog, usually a hound.

breed (n.). Dogs developed by humans to meet specific criteria in looks and traits.

breed club (n.). An organization dedicated to a particular breed of dog.

breed standard (n.). A written description of a specific breed of dog that contains all of the criteria a dog must meet.

brisket (n.). The part of dog's body between the front legs and between the neck and the ribs.

canine teeth (n.). The long teeth just outside the incisors.

carpus (n.). The bones in a dog's skeleton that are comparable to the human wrist.

castrate (v.). To surgically remove the testicles of a male animal.

cesarean section (n.). Surgery to remove the puppies from a pregnant animal.

character (n.). The individual personality traits of a dog.

chest (n.). The part of the body enclosed by the ribs.

condition (n.). The dog's state of health and being.

conformation (n.). The structure and form of the individual dog.

congenital (adj.). Inherited.

contagious (adj.). Capable of being spread from one animal to another by air or contact.

coprophagia (n.). The act of eating feces.

coursing (n.). The sport of chasing game.

crest (n.). The top of head; or, the hair on top of the head.

cropped (v.). To trim a dog's ears.

cross breed (n.). A dog whose parents are pure-bred dogs of different breeds.

croup (n.). The part of the dog's back just in front of the tail.

dewclaw (n.). The claw on the inside of the dog's leg.

dewlap (n.). Hanging skin under the throat.

diatomaceous earth (n.). A chalky, powder-like substance used as a natural pest-control product.

disqualification (n.). A condition that makes a dog ineligible to compete.

dock (v.). To remove all or part of a dog's tail.

dog (n.). A male of the dog family.

dominance (n.). The position of leadership in a pack of dogs.

double coat (n.). The coat of a dog, such as an Alaskan Malamute, that has soft under hairs and a longer overcoat.

ear leather (n.). The skin of a dog's ear.

estrus (n.). The part of a female's reproductive cycle when she is receptive to the male.

euthanize (v.). To end the life of an animal, usually by injection.

express (v.). To apply pressure in order to force out the contents.

flews (n.). Hanging upper lips.

gait (n.). The pattern of how an animal moves its one foot in conjunction with the other.

game (n.). A wild animal hunted for food or sport.

gene (n.). An element that carries characteristics that are inherited from the father and mother.

group (n.). A set of dog breeds that all share similar main traits.

hackles (n.). The hairs on the head, neck, and shoulders that are raised when a dog is angry or afraid.

heartworm (n.). A parasite that invades a dog's heart.

heat (n.). The part of the estrus cycle of a female dog when she is ready to mate with a male.

hip dysplasia (n.). A condition of a dog's hips that causes degenerative disease.

hocks (n.). The bones in a dog's hind leg that form the ankle.

hormone (n.). A substance produced in the body to stimulate certain functions, sometimes related to mating.

immunization (n.). An injection of medicine to help protect an animal from certain diseases.

impacted (adj.). Packed together so that an opening is blocked.

inbred (adj.). Born of parents that are closely related.

incision (n.). A cut made during surgery.

incisors (n.). The front teeth of a dog between the canine teeth.

instinct (n.). A behavior that is present at birth and not learned.

kennel club (n.). An organization that maintains records of the dogs of a certain breed.

labor (n.). The process of giving birth.

larva (n.). The immature, worm-like stage in the life cycle of some insects.

line bred (adj.). Born of parents that are related, but the relationship is at least one generation removed.

loin (n.). The part of a dog's body between the ribs and the croup.

marrow (n.). The soft tissue found inside bones.

mat splitter (n.). A grooming tool with a sharp blade used to cut apart matted hair.

mixed breed (n.). A dog whose parents are not of the same breed or are mixed breed.

molar (n.). The grinding teeth in the rear of the mouth.

mongrel (n.). A mixed breed dog.

mouthing (v.). A dog's habit of placing its mouth around part of the body of another dog or a person.

mutt (n.). A mixed breed dog.

muzzle (n.). The part of a dog's head from the nose to the eyes.

neuter (v.). To make an animal unable to breed.

nose leather (n.). The portion of a dog's nose that is not covered by fur.

occiput (n.). The part of the skull found at the upper back.

ovary (n.). The part of a female's reproductive system that produces eggs.

overcoat (n.). The second or top coat on double-coated dogs.

pastern (n.). The group of bones between the feet and carpus.

pedigree (n.). The written ancestry of a dog.

pica (n.). The practice of eating non-food items, such as paper or plastic.

placenta (n.). An organ that develops in pregnant animals by which unborn babies are attached to the uterus.

puberty (n.). The age at which an animal becomes physically capable of producing offspring.

pure breed (n.). A dog whose parents are of the same breed.

recessive (adj.). Hidden, as a genetic trait.

registered (adj.). Listed with a kennel club.

scent hound (n.). A type of dog that tracks or follows a trail using its sense of smell.

scent marking (v.). The act of leaving scent as a territorial indicator.

scrotum (n.). The external sac that contains the testicles of a male animal.

secretion (n.). A substance released from an animal's body.

selective breeding (n.). The practice of choosing animals to mate in order to produce young that have certain characteristics.

selvage (n.). The edge of a fabric that is woven so that it will not ravel.

shock (n.). A body's reacton to severe injury or disease in which some physical functions slow down or stop.

sight hound (n.). A type of dog that tracks or follows game using its sense of sight.

smooth coat (n.). Short hair lying flat against a dog's body.

spay (v.). To neuter a female dog.

splay feet (n.). Feet on which the toes are spread apart.

stifle (n.). The rounded front portion of the rear leg between the body and the hock.

stop (n.). The angle from the muzzle to the skull.

testicles (n.). The glands in a male dog that produce sperm.

thoroughbred (n.). A term sometimes used to describe a purebred dog.

tracking (v.). Following a trail using the sense of smell.

undercoat (n.). The first coat of a double-coated breed — usually found in winter.

uterus (n.). The organ in the body of a female where babies develop when she is pregnant.

vulva (n.). The external opening to the genital tract of a female.

whelp (v., n.). The act of giving birth; or, the name for a young puppy.

wire hair (n.). Hair with a hard texture.

withers (n.). The top of the shoulders.

Index

Page references in *italic* indicate illustrations; **bold** indicates charts.